Never Say Never

Never Say Never

*A TV Producer & Pig Farmer's
Love Story of Faith,
Resilience and Business Success*

LISA KROEHLER

Copyright © 2024
Lisa Kroehler

Performance Publishing
McKinney, TX

All Worldwide Rights Reserved.

All rights reserved. No part of this publication may be reproduced, stored in a retrieval system or transmitted, in any form or by any means, electronic, mechanical, recorded, photocopied, or otherwise, without the prior written permission of the copyright owner, except by a reviewer who may quote brief passages in a review.

ISBN: 978-1-961781-40-5 paperback
ISBN: 978-1-961781-36-8 hardcover

For my husband Keith: Thank you for your steadfast love through it all.

To my children Jessica, Josh, and Justin: These true stories are for you and future generations. Dad and I love you.

PRAISE FOR NEVER SAY NEVER

"As entrepreneurs-we often feel alone. Reading Lisa's book, I couldn't help but smile and take comfort in the simple truth- we are NOT alone. It is a beautifully written story of Lisa and her husband Keith's struggles, triumphs, centered around their faith and the refusal to give up. I'm immensely proud of Lisa for putting in the work to memorialize one family's amazingly crazy story - that will inspire any entrepreneur who reads it."

-Brandon Vaughn
Serial Entrepreneur; CEO, HireBus

"Imagine starting a family and business at a time before the internet, home service CRMs, and QuickBooks. Lisa Kroehler doesn't have to imagine it because she lived it. This is her story. ***Never Say Never*** is engaging, real, and sometimes a little raw. Learn how a pig farmer and television producer teamed up to start a window cleaning business...and were met with success by God's grace. Learn how they did it and be inspired that you can do it, too. As Lisa says: "This is how many small businesses start: a little start-up capital, no bells or whistles, just hard work and a dream." As an added bonus, Lisa's Takeaways for Life at the end of every chapter makes it easy to put into practice the lesson learned."

-Dan Holland
CEO, Droplet International, Inc.

"Lisa and Keith are the real deal. They are authentic, have strong character, and a heart for people. Their love and entrepreneurial story is an inspiration to the home services industry. Anyone and everyone who knows them will recommend picking up this book!"

-Mike Dahlke
Booyah Capital Partners

"What sets this book apart is its refreshing authenticity. Getting to know the romantic story of two legacy entrepreneurs is unique and intimate. There are no gimmicks or shortcuts here—just honest, hard-earned wisdom gleaned from years of experience. Whether you're a seasoned veteran or just starting out in the home service industry, **Never Say Never** serves as a beacon of hope and a reminder that with dedication and perseverance, anything is possible."

-Whitney White
CEO, Wise Coatings Franchises

"I love a good story, and **Never Say Never** is the true story of Lisa and Keith's fantastic journey of the ups and downs of marriage, business, and faith that led them to a prosperous life of serving their community, family, and Lord. I have not only read this story but was there to see much of it unfold over my years of knowing this amazing couple. I know Lisa's journey will provide laughs and encouragement and be a guide to trust when an opportunity comes out of left field; you should never say never!"

-John P. Ondo
Filmmaker/Media Influencer

"Lisa's story is not what you would expect from observing the thriving and successful IDW company today. After reading Keith and Lisa's story, my respect for them has only deepened and emboldened my journey as a follower of Jesus and a leader with an entrepreneurial spirit. Lisa weaves authenticity, humility, grit, perseverance, failures, growth, hard decisions, faith, and obedience into a beautiful picture of what only God can do! You will savor the truth that God does not waste anything and faithfully provides when we obediently walk with Him, that threads throughout their story! "

-**Kari D. Taylor, LPCC-S**
Executive Director, Cornerstone of Hope Lima

In her book, **Never Say Never**, Lisa Kroehler shares her life and love story with her husband, Keith. She is a good storyteller, and you feel like you are walking right along beside her. Lisa explains how her faith in God is woven in and out of all the seasons of her life, and how perseverance and listening to the Lord will bring you through. This book relates to the ups and downs life brings for couples and business owners.

-**Karen Lockyer**
Owner, SoftWash Systems

I have journeyed with Lisa as her pastor, serving together as board members, watching her as a leader worth following, and best of all, as a friend. In this, I have witnessed the reality of Lisa & Keith's faith and perseverance. **Never Say Never** is a great find. It superbly inspires, infuses wisdom to overcome the worst, as well as re-ignites the trust that with God all things are possible.

-**Dr. Dan Huckins**
Senior Leadership Consultant
GiANT Worldwide

"My wife, Terri and I have been friends with Lisa and Keith for over 30 years and consider them some of our dearest friends. We have watched first-hand how they have trusted and relied fully on God. Their marriage is built on the foundation of Jesus Christ, and has produced amazing children and grandchildren, and has stood the test of many trials. Their business has defied the statistics of new start-up business failures, and today is one of the most respected businesses in its industry. Their undying love for each other, the Lord, their family, friends and their business are the Hallmark of Lisa and Keith. I'm certain you will enjoy."

-Brent D. Stechschulte
Vice President of Corporate Services,
Tuttle Services Inc.

"It is a common belief that when people from different backgrounds or cultures meet and marry, their differences collide. My life experience teaches me that this is not true. Watching "The Pig Farmer" and "The TV Producer" work together, struggle together, and ultimately succeed together as a couple, as parents, and as business partners has been a joy. You should read this story in book form. It is sure to encourage, to entertain, and most of all to inspire."

-Robert Sielschott
Author, Founding Father: The Lost Essays;
President, SWKRS CPA's, Inc.

"In a whirlwind of adventure, faith, and resilience, ***Never Say Never*** is more than a captivating tale or business memoir. It is a true story of a faith-filled couple who discover real success isn't measured by financial wealth alone but by the strength of their bond and the depth of their convictions in God. Keith and Lisa's journey inspires belief in the power of love and perseverance. You are sure to feel encouraged to embrace challenges and pursue your dreams!"

-Lori Bucher
Co-Lead Pastor, Lima First Church

"Embark on an inspiring journey with ***Never Say Never***, the captivating tale of a pig farmer and TV producer. This memoir weaves faith, resilience, and love into a powerful narrative, offering a beacon of hope for those facing life's challenges. More than just a personal story, it's a guide for navigating life's complexities. This emotionally gripping book is a must-read that proves anything is possible when embracing faith and an open heart. It is a story of triumph over adversity, summarizing the power of resilience and the boundless possibilities that unfold when we dare to believe."

-Paul Swartz
President, Swartz Restoration & Emergency Services

Never Say Never is a beautiful story of the entrepreneurial journey. Running a business requires hard work, determination, and discipline if you are going to be successful. Lisa and Keith's story will inspire and encourage current and future entrepreneurs in their journey.

-Tim O'Neil
Certified Entrepreneurial Operating System Coach

"My elementary school friend has discovered the truth that real success—both in business and in life-- depends on commitment to core values of perseverance, faithfulness, and integrity. Whether you make your living as part of a global conglomerate or on your own, Lisa and Keith's story will inspire you to stay true to Godly principles as you face setbacks and uncertainties in your own journey."

-**Lisa Wurster**
Vice President and Assistant General Counsel, Dana Incorporated

"Decades ago, as a broadcasting colleague, I witnessed firsthand the unfolding of this true and engaging story. It's about two people who through years of hard work and sacrifice, along with their faith in a miracle-working God, overcame countless obstacles to achieve the American dream.

If you need inspiration for your own God-given vision or simply enjoy a heartwarming and incredibly well-written book, then this is a must read.

I'm hoping to see this overcoming all the odds story on the big screen in the near future. It would make a powerful and uplifting movie."

-**Christina Ryan Claypool**
Former TV Producer/Reporter and National Amy award-winning freelance journalist

CONTENTS

Chapter 1: Love at Sea 1

Chapter 2: Tossed To and From 19

Chapter 3: In the Rearview Mirror 33

Chapter 4: Green Acres - Life on the Farm*- 49

Chapter 5: Chasing the Wind 63

Chapter 6: Failure - Part of the Formula 81

Chapter 7: Take Two: Starting Over 93

Chapter 8: Together We Can 109

Chapter 9: Seize the Day 119

Chapter 10: Counting the Costs 131

Chapter 11: A Life of Gratitude 149

CHAPTER 1

LOVE AT SEA

I looked down the hallway and saw band members with multi-colored hair, neon clothing, and an 80s pop music vibe. They didn't look like that in their publicity photos!

I was the telethon producer at a small Christian television station in Ohio. Our conservative audience really liked Southern Gospel music, but I wanted to give a fresh change to our nightly "live" music. I stumbled upon a young Christian rock band named Bash-n-the-Code (formerly Found Free) out of Philadelphia. I could book them for very little money. The station director gave me permission to bring them in. I am so glad I had permission!

Telethons were how nonprofit Christian stations raised funding. That particular spring, the telethon took forty-eight straight days of on-air talking and music before we met our goal. After seeing the band, I was wondering if I would lose my job over hiring them. The station manager called me into his office. I fully expected him to tell me they could not go on the air that night.

"I imagine you have seen the band by now?" he calmly asked.

All I could do was nod and say, "They look so different from their photos. I am so sorry."

He paused for a minute, drawing out the agony I felt.

"I think we should give them a chance," he surprisingly said. "I know we'll take some flak from some viewers, but let's have them sing a couple of songs and see what happens."

I was shocked! My respect for this man grew greatly. He was sticking his neck out on "live" television for a band that was definitely going to generate phone calls but probably not raise money.

That night a miracle took place. The band members started sharing their testimonies of how Christ had changed their lives. The phones were ringing—people were praying with counselors, and lives were being changed. It became clear this was a God-ordained moment, and we were all part of it. And those that complained? Some called back later and apologized for judging the band on their appearance only. What a lesson to all of us.

When we were off the air, the band's lead singer told my roommate, Leesa, and me about a singles cruise they were sponsoring in July. A Caribbean cruise featuring music by their band and other well-known contemporary Christian artists. He wanted us to be part of the media on the cruise. We still had to come up with the money to sail away. But the idea of a vacation, let alone on a cruise ship, was exhilarating. But how would we come up with the money? We could barely keep up with our rent and car repairs.

A few days after the telethon, I casually mentioned the cruise to Mom. She loved watching telethons and enjoyed the band. Immediately, she offered to loan me the money for the trip. What? My parents didn't have much money, especially after raising six children in a one-income household. Dad worked most of his life on the engine line at Ford Motor Company.

"Mom, I am not asking you to lend me that money," I protested.

"Well, you didn't ask me," she said. "I offered it, and there's a difference."

Mom was a forthright, strong-willed woman—definitely not a pushover. And yet she was every bit a servant in our home. My earliest remembrances are of her cooking, not only for all of us but also for her teenage stepbrothers, Ted and Terry. Their dad was a long haul truck driver who was seldom home. I didn't know all the details, but life was tough since their mom (my grandmother) died in her fifties. My step-grandpa married a couple of women after her, but their mother was gone.

My mom did what she could to make life a little better for them. Mom's dinner specialties were pot roast, green beans, and mashed potatoes, or beef and noodles, mashed potatoes, and baked beans. Somehow she made a tight budget go pretty far.

I couldn't wait to tell Leesa that Mom offered to lend me the money for the cruise.

"Maybe this is meant to be," I told her excitedly. "Maybe it's our destiny to go on this ship and meet someone. Our lives could be changed by this trip!"

> *"Maybe it's our destiny to go on this ship and meet someone. Our lives could be changed by this trip!"*

Leesa liked that idea. "I'm going to call my mom too and tell her about the cruise. I am not going to ask for the money, but If she offers to loan it to me, then we will know that this is a present from God!"

Leesa's mom said the same thing that my mom did! Maybe both were secretly wishing they were going on the cruise. Or maybe they were feeling a little desperate for their single daughters!

The next couple of months were spent planning our upcoming summer trip. Leesa was twenty-eight and an outgoing, attractive person who never seemed to have a problem getting dates. I always seemed to attract men I was not interested in. Being on local television, some people did see you as a local celebrity. I think that was because we were not reading scripts. We were on talk shows and programs like telethons where you actually got to share from the heart.

People felt like they knew you personally. I sometimes received dating proposals in the mail. Other times, I had single men come to a "live" broadcast to meet me after the show. Yes, it all was very awkward and made both Leesa and me realize that there were a lot of lonely people out there searching for the right person.

A Personal Portrait

Let me say that I was not a fashion model. I was tall, thin, and blonde, but I always considered myself more of a tomboy than anything else. Of course, I dressed up on television and had to wear lots of makeup under the bright lights. I learned quickly that you are fair game for everyone's opinions about how you should look. I had women follow me in clothing stores and hide behind the racks just to tell me that I wear the wrong colors on television.

I did not know there was such a thing as a seasonal color analysis. I found that other women care more about your hairstyle than your clothes and are eager to give you suggestions. This television spotlight was new territory and a lot different than just penning your byline on a newspaper article. With that said, the sweet part was when a viewer shared how their life had been drastically changed through a testimonial story we had produced or when we interviewed someone whose disastrous life had been turned around by the love of Christ. That is what really mattered to me.

I was getting used to the ups and downs of being on television when a man named Ray wrote me a letter to say he was in love with me. We had never met. Ray was a fan of our station who had convinced himself that he and I were meant for each other. Ray sent me many detailed letters over a period of a couple of months. He referred to my ministry segments where I would make statements such as, "You are loved" or "I really care about your life."

I, of course, was speaking in general terms, referring to God wanting to have a relationship with each of us. Ray was probably fifteen years older than me and lived with his parents on a farm. He took my words as a secret message to him.

A handwriting analyst would probably say that he was a troubled man. His letters would change from print to cursive, from capital letters to tiny letters, all in the same sentence. His words sounded like a teen's first love letter. Then suddenly, he would refer to an unsolved murder of a girl on his country road. He made creepy statements about this girl that made me wonder whether I should contact the authorities. The letters usually mentioned, "I never want something like that to happen to you."

> *Then suddenly, he would refer to an unsolved murder of a girl on his country road.*

One night, I was working alone at the TV station, and I heard someone in the hallway. I thought it was the Master Control Operator and called out to him from my office. There was no response. I walked to the doorway and slowly peeked around the corner. My heart was beating faster, and my palms were sweaty. There he was!

Ray was a short, balding man with wire-rimmed glasses. I recognized him from when he had recently surprised me at my church. After weeks of getting his letters, he sat behind me on a Sunday morning. During the greeting time, he simply said, "Hi. I am Ray." My stomach sank to my feet that morning in church. But that night, he was invading my private world, and I was alone.

"Hi! Lisa," he said, then shyly looked downward. I suddenly felt a surge of boldness. I was close to six feet tall in heels, and I was not going to succumb to fear.

"Ray, what are you doing in here?" I said, raising my voice. "You shouldn't be here. I really want you to leave now!"

I was breathing hard in a panic and hustled past him to the outside door. I hoped he would follow me. I didn't have a game plan, but I needed to show him that I was strong. He started rambling about how sorry he was that he had startled me. He told me that I meant a lot to him, and he wanted to be around me.

"Ray, you need to move on with your life. We are not meant to be together. You have taken my words on television out of context. It is God you need, not me. We are not a couple," I firmly said.

For just a moment, I felt sorry for him. He obviously had problems. But I could not take pity on him. I was a single woman, all alone. I had no idea of his mental state. This is how stories have bad endings, and I did not want mine to end that way. Ray looked downward as he walked slowly out the door toward his pink Cadillac. I knew he was dejected, but he seemed to accept what I had said.

I bolted the door shut and made sure he got in his car. Then I ran down the hall with tears streaming down my face. I thanked God for his protection and surge of courage. To an outsider, I may have seemed a little harsh. But after weeks of stalking, I knew this was what I had to do and say. The next day, I took all his letters to the local sheriff's department. I never heard from Ray again, and I do not know what happened to him. I can only pray that he found peace in his life.

All Aboard

The Caribbean cruise was an answer to my prayers. Not only did I need some fun in my life, but I also needed to feel good about myself. I was struggling with who I was and where I was going. Spiritually, I was doing well, but as a single woman, I was wondering if I would ever meet someone who could love and understand me.

I was independent. I liked to think outside of the box and try risky adventures. That's probably why I had chosen newspaper and television as careers. I had covered stories in a hot air balloon (which ended in a crash) and a Life Flight helicopter. I had traveled on the road with a truck driver, reported in an Abrams army tank, and had done investigative work in a couple of questionable establishments. (Sorry, Mom).

I was only twenty-five and had already met a lifetime of interesting people and shared their stories. Now, here

I was on a cruise ship, wondering if there was another story worth covering. Maybe this time, it would be my story with an amazing ending.

On this sunny Sunday afternoon, we were sailing out of Tampa/St. Pete on Commodore Cruise Line's MS Boheme dubbed "The Happy Ship." Our first port would be Key West, FL, then Jamaica, the Grand Cayman Islands, and Cozumel, Mexico. I was ecstatic at the thought of visiting these amazing paradises. Canada was the farthest country I had been to, and it was not tropical!

From the moment Leesa and I boarded the ship, I felt like royalty. The politeness of the sharply-dressed crew and the food delicacies we tried even before we had left port were just the beginning of an enchanted trip. I had never been exposed to anything like this.

Compared to today's luxury liners, the Boheme was a small ship, only 440 feet long. It held a maximum of 540 passengers. Other than that, my only real knowledge of cruise ships came from what I had learned on the television show *The Love Boat*. But what really made this trip unique was hearing and mingling with the 1980s Contemporary Christian singers onboard, like Russ Taff, Randy Stonehill, and Phil Keaggy. They, along with the cruise sponsors, Bash-n-the-Code, would be singing in the evenings.

NEVER SAY NEVER

A Love Story Unfolds

On the second night, I met Keith Kroehler. "Hi, I'm Keith," a well-tanned, muscular man said as we were standing in the hallway waiting for the concert doors to open. "I saw the band introduce you last night. Being on television must be an exciting life."

I knew I was blushing. I am not sure if it was because he thought my life was more glamorous than it really was or because he was handsome, and I felt a little intimidated. I couldn't help but notice the dimples when he smiled.

"Yes, it's a good fit for me," I said awkwardly. "So, what do you do for a living?"

"Oh, I'm a pig farmer from Minnesota," he boldly told me.

I never would have guessed that. I fully expected him to say he was in sales or maybe even a business executive. Granted, I was making that judgment in a split second of meeting him, but I was impressed that he was a proud farmer.

"Well, that certainly isn't something I hear every day. I guess you could say you are an agricultural engineer," I laughed, trying to figure out where to go with this conversation. Maybe I offended him. But Keith wasn't fazed by my comment at all. He continued to talk about the cruise and asked me lots of questions.

There was something very calm and easygoing about him, but at the same time, he was quite inquisitive. He had a chiseled physique and dark hair. He was confident but not cocky... and obviously very physically strong. I imagine that he would have to be tough to wrestle pigs. At least, that's what he said he had to do from time to time.

> *I imagine that he would have to be tough to wrestle pigs. At least, that's what he said he had to do from time to time.*

Keith told me he had come on the cruise alone to celebrate his twenty-ninth birthday. Who does that alone? He talked about the long days on the farm and how difficult it was to get away from work. He and his father operated the farm, which included more than raising pigs. There was equipment to fix, pens to clean, pigs to castrate, and others to breed, plus fences and buildings to repair and maintain, hay to bale, and the list goes on. I definitely could not ever imagine doing any of that in my lifetime.

Keith told me he was looking through a Christian magazine one day and saw the singles cruise advertised. He decided that it was the perfect vacation. He never even thought about finding a friend to go with him.

Immediately, I was interested in getting to know this guy better. His adventurous spirit and calm demeanor intrigued me. After talking for several minutes, I decided to take a bold step.

"Keith, uh, when we get to Jamaica tomorrow, are you going on an excursion?" I started feeling a little self-conscious. "Uh, it's okay if you already have one scheduled, but I just thought that if you didn't, maybe you would like to go with me on the bamboo raft trip?"

I was really sounding desperate for a date.

"I would love to," Keith said eagerly. "Let's sign up!"

First Date in Paradise

Our day on the river together was so much fun. The few-hour trip on the Rio Grande, one of Jamaica's longest rivers, started with us sitting on an elevated "loveseat" on a twenty-foot bamboo raft. A skilled raft captain guided us down the river with a long bamboo pole. The hot sun was shining, and we stopped a couple of times to get into the water to cool off.

I was not a fan of swimming in a brown river. I wondered what else was swimming underneath the surface. At the end of the afternoon, we walked along the banks of the river, sharing about our lives and laughing about our different backgrounds.

Keith was distracted when he saw a Jamaican man roasting some kind of meat over a fire. Without hesitation, he gladly gave him money to try this unknown meat. He must have an iron gut, I remember thinking. No other passenger was remotely interested in trying that food. Keith definitely defied boundaries. Was he always up for a challenge?

After our day in Jamaica, we spent most of the other days on the cruise together. There were disco parties, themed dress up parties like Christmas in July, sixties night, Christian concerts, talent shows, sun tanning, food tasting, chocolate fountains, and, of course, excursions to other ports. But there were also times when I could not find Keith because he was sleeping in the middle of the day.

For him, part of the vacation was about rest. He worked physically hard all the time, and this trip was a welcome respite. I had no understanding of that at the time—I could only see the turquoise water and hear the tropical music calling my name.

Our time in Cozumel, Mexico, was a real turning point. It was the sixth night of the cruise, and our time together was coming to an end. I did not want it to. We were sitting under a palm tree, talking very seriously for a couple of hours. He was so different from the other men I had met.

Transparency. Expression. Honesty. He freely talked about his life and the hardships his family had been through.

His mother died of cancer at age fifty-two, just a couple of years before we met. Keith had quit college and football to return to the family farm. The farm operation was financially strapped, and he and his father worked relentlessly to hold onto it. I could tell that Keith was a man of integrity with an impeccable work ethic. He shared every detail and even talked through tears at times.

He shared his growing faith in God and his desire to marry a Christian woman and raise children who love God. I knew in my heart that this guy was for real. He was not trying to win me over. This was not an act of desperation. He was bearing his soul.

> *I knew in my heart that this guy was for real. He was not trying to win me over. This was not an act of desperation. He was bearing his soul.*

My heart was leaping. Could this be the man I had always prayed about? The man I was meant to be with? Is it possible to fall in love with someone so quickly?

The cruise ended, and most people stayed one more night at the Tradewinds Hotel on St. Pete Beach. Keith and I walked the beach that night and talked about how we could stay connected despite our ten-hour distance. This was way before cell phones, texting, and FaceTime. We knew that long-distance phone calls and writing letters would be important but difficult. The moon glowed over the ocean that night; it was the most romantic setting I had ever been in. We sat on a grassy hill next to the beach, looking in awe at the stars.

As a journalist, my life was about asking questions and digging deeper. This whirlwind romance on a cruise ship really rocked my voice of reason. Neither of us wanted to be hasty in a relationship, but we both believed that God could orchestrate two people meeting and falling in love. I knew there was a lot that would have to happen before I could really say that I loved this man. But I knew there was potential in our relationship, and that gave me great hope.

The next day, we sat in a diner, saying our last goodbyes. We talked about how we could stay connected 700 miles apart and both agreed that the feelings we already had for each other were real. Neither of us believed that this was just a romantic fling on a Caribbean vacation. Suddenly, his airport bus pulled in sooner than we had planned.

"I have to go!" he shrieked, jumped up, and grabbed his suitcase. He pulled me close and kissed me goodbye. Then he held me in his arms for what seemed like forever but really was only seconds.

He ran out the door, and as he stepped onto the bus, he turned and looked my way to smile. Watching the bus drive off made me feel like I was living in a black-and-white movie. I was left standing there alone, wondering if I would ever see him again.

LISA KROEHLER

TAKEAWAYS FOR LIFE

I had been compiling my spouse checklist for a long time. Of course, I wanted to marry a strong Christian man, but I also saw myself with someone in a white-collar profession. Meeting Keith challenged my preconceived ideas. Does a person's career choice really matter in a relationship? Obviously, there is way more to a man's character than what he does for a living. In the Bible, God emphasizes love, kindness, compassion, patience, truthfulness, and faithfulness. If a man is living the opposite of it, we should run fast.

I knew that God wanted me to pair up with someone who would inspire me, challenge me to be a better person, and strengthen my relationship with Christ. I was attracted to Keith physically but also attracted to him spiritually because I saw Godly characteristics in him.

The bigger question now was not about him as a person but how we would ever develop this long-distance relationship. In current times, that is not as much of a problem. But thirty-eight years ago, it was challenging. No cell phones or internet, and we both had limited income. I knew that faith and trust would be very important in this new adventure.

Would it last long? Could it last a lifetime? I wanted to believe that the best was yet to come.

CHAPTER 2

TOSSED TO AND FROM

My heart and mind were all over the place when I left Florida. On the airplane, my mind relived all of the moments and deep conversations we had. When Keith hurriedly ran to catch his bus, he left my contact information laying on the table. I did have his address, though. Should I write to him immediately? I did not want to be pushy, but I knew that if I did not make a strong effort to connect pretty quickly, this would just be a vacation romance. I wanted something more than that.

A few days after I was home, I sent him a short, friendly, unromantic letter. I mostly talked about the wonderful vacation and chatted about upcoming television projects I was working on. I did make it clear that I would love to hear from him, and I included my phone number. Then I waited to see what would happen next.

Within a couple of days, he called, and that was the beginning of our long-distance relationship. I learned quickly that handwritten letters take time and require more thought than just speaking on the phone. But if a relationship is worth pursuing, you make the effort. Both of us did in our own way.

Keith was creative in the notes he sent. They were actually gifts. There was a piece of wood with a cute poem written on it. The red frisbee with a "Come fly away with me" romantic note written in black marker. And the plastic pumpkin hanging on my mailbox with a sweet note written on the inside. None of these were in boxes. The mailman delivered them just as they were. I am sure that the neighbors noticed the unusual mail sticking out of my mailbox on Primrose Place.

By the end of the summer, I had been to Minnesota twice—once with my roommate, Leesa, who was from Minneapolis, and once alone. That does not sound like much time, but we did have a few days together on each trip. Most of our time was spent talking or doing something outdoors to get to know each other better. I briefly met his dad and a couple of his sisters.

You could tell that they really cared about their brother, and I am sure they felt a little protective of him.

After all, he had just met a stranger on a ship, and now he was bringing her to meet the family. Even though we were just at the beginning of our relationship, I tried to imagine myself living around Henderson. Would I fit in? What would I do for a living?

Now it was October, and Keith was coming to meet my family for the first time. He drove his truck and trailer to Indiana to deliver pigs, then drove through the night to Lima, Ohio. After a few hours at my parents' house, I remember Mom privately saying to me, "I think this guy has probably checked all of the boxes on your list."

They especially loved that Keith was inquisitive, decisive, and self-motivated. He even pitched in on dish washing and hauling firewood. But I was still pondering whether this relationship could work long term.

Our weekends together always went by so fast. I had a lot on my mind as we turned the corner into Sunday. We were walking hand in hand along Primrose Place, but we were not talking. The rustling of the October leaves blowing across the road helped break the silence. He knew that I had a lot on my mind and was about to say something that could be life-changing for him. It had been a whirlwind three months, and most of it was exciting and unpredictable.

LISA KROEHLER

The Aftermath

I really had fallen fast for this man. I loved getting to know him the best I could, considering the distance. But reality was pressing hard against me. Was this just a romantic love story that really can't have a happy ending? We were from such different worlds—he a pig farmer and me a television producer. With a ten-hour distance, could we ever really get to know each other well? How do you ever bridge such a gap? And did I really want to?

But reality was pressing hard against me. Was this just a romantic love story that really can't have a happy ending?

"Keith," I quietly said while holding his hand tighter. "I really need to share some thoughts that are mulling around in my mind all of the time."

The wind picked up and blew the leaves in circles—kind of how I was feeling at that moment. He stared ahead and simply said, "Okay." He squeezed my hand hard.

I took a deep breath and started talking.

"I really think I am falling in love with you. There are so many wonderful things about you that I have always looked for in a man. But there are so many things that I just can't figure out. I don't think I can give up my career and move to your farm. Gosh, I am not a farm girl," I confessed, trying to imagine myself smelling the pigs all of the time. "I don't know how I would adapt, and I've certainly never lived that far from my family."

Keith did not respond right away. He was always good at contemplating before speaking—not my strength. We definitely were opposites in so many ways. I know they say that opposites attract, but where do you draw the line on your differences? Fortunately, our faith and even our political views lined up, but I always had high aspirations for my career. What would I do if I moved to a farm? I was still trying to wrap my mind around that lifestyle, although my heart definitely was wrapped around him.

"I want the best for your life, Lisa," Keith started to say. "I have prayed for a long time for someone like you. There is so much about you that I love, even though we are very different. I think we can complement each other and have a wonderful life together. But you know that I can't leave the farm." He turned to me and pulled me close. "Right now, I just can't. Please, don't make a decision about me just yet. Keep praying on it. I don't want to lose you."

As I looked into his eyes, I could see that he was fighting tears. I resisted the urge to kiss him because I did not want to be misleading. I was confused. My thoughts about possibly ending the relationship had nothing to do with how I felt about him now. I had only known him a short time, and maintaining a long-distance relationship was challenging.

It was more about knowing that I would eventually have to move to Minnesota and live on a farm. That probably seems shallow, but it was a big mountain for me. We walked back to my Cape Cod house and said our goodbyes. I had a knot in my stomach as I hugged him. Was I overthinking all of the details? Was this relationship the best for my life? I did not know the answers at this point. I watched Keith drive away in his truck. I found out later that he cried most of the trip back to Minnesota.

Although I was not ready to commit long term, I also was not ready to say that it was over. I definitely was battling my fear of the unknown. I was afraid to leave the comfortable life I had always known and the same people I had always been around. The thought of leaving everything and everyone behind was daunting. My parents and my four brothers and sister all lived nearby.

That said, I was drawn to Keith. There was so much about him that made sense to me. He was the type of man I had been looking for. My heart and mind were in a tug of war. For the time being, he was willing to put up with my doubts and questions. But how long could that go on?

NEVER SAY NEVER

Love Is A Decision

My roommate was driving to Minneapolis for Thanksgiving. This was the ideal time for me to tag along and spend more time with Keith. Fortunately, we arrived there before a snowstorm hit. I was standing in Keith's farm kitchen looking out the window at twenty-six inches of snow. I don't think I had seen that much snow on the ground since the Blizzard of 1978. This was not unusual, though, for Minnesota.

"I could never live here," I blurted out as I watched the blowing snow. Immediately, Keith's face fell. Once again, I was voicing my doubt about a long-term relationship.

After we returned to Ohio, I decided to do some deep soul-searching and praying. Instead of just thinking about all of the challenges facing our relationship, I needed to really understand what love was. I read scripture after scripture about love. I read books about love and marriage. I talked with one of my pastors to get some godly wisdom. I learned that love is a choice that requires hard decisions and sacrifices. The world tries to make it all about romance and fulfilling everything that we personally desire, but it is far deeper than that.

Was I willing to sacrifice my career and where I lived for someone I believed I loved? Was I willing to start my life over from scratch? That was the turning point in our relationship. God brought me to my knees, and I surrendered all of my doubts and fears to Him. I could not see the bigger picture, but my Lord could. I felt a peace overcome me like I had never had to that degree. I knew now that, beyond a shadow of a doubt, this man was someone I wanted to spend the rest of my life with. I believed that God had brought us together in the middle of an ocean for something greater than we could ever imagine.

Unexpected Route

Now it was April of 1986, and I was flying to Minneapolis for Keith's sister's wedding. A man I had known for a while and had casually gone on a few dates with before I had met Keith offered to drive me to the airport. On the way, he unexpectedly veered into a community park.

"Where are we going, Mack?" I asked, bewildered. "I don't want to miss my plane."

He pulled over and asked me to get out of the car. I suddenly felt nervous. Mack grabbed a blanket out of the back seat; now I was feeling very uncom-

> *I suddenly felt nervous. Mack grabbed a blanket out of the back seat; now I was feeling very uncomfortable.*

fortable. He laid the blanket down on the hillside, and I reluctantly sat down.

"Lisa, I know we haven't dated a lot, but now is the time to tell you how I feel. I am in love with you and want to marry you," Mack said very seriously. He pulled out a large diamond ring and tried to put it on my finger. Of course, I resisted.

"Mack, I am so surprised by this. You know how I feel about Keith. I hope I didn't give you the wrong impression, but this just isn't right." I stood up.

"I am on my way to see him, and I believe he is the right man for me," I insisted.

"Lisa, please tell me that you will think about it. Take the ring with you and promise me you will think about it," he pleaded.

There was no way I was going to be responsible for a diamond ring that I didn't even want. I refused and firmly asked him to take me to the airport. When we got back in the car, he popped open the glove compartment and pulled out two airline tickets.

"We could just fly to Florida right now and get married. I have the tickets," he announced eagerly.

I was dumbfounded. Was this really happening right now? The only thing I could think to say was that I didn't have Florida clothes. I had Minnesota clothes packed.

Yes, I know that was a dumb response, but I was totally improvising.

He countered with, "I'll buy you a new wardrobe when we get there."

"Mack, take me to the airport. This is not happening. You are a nice guy, but I am not in love with you. I am in love with Keith."

Reluctantly, he took me to the airport, and there was one more surprise. He took a dozen red roses out of the backseat and handed them to me. "Please think about it; that is all I am asking."

I was totally caught off guard and did not know how I was supposed to act in this situation. I thanked Mack for the roses but did not get near him as I quickly walked down the jetway to the plane. I was shaking. I could not believe what had just happened. I took the roses on the plane but ended up handing them out to the passengers when we landed. I did not want Keith to see me carrying flowers from another man… and certainly not carrying a diamond ring.

When I deplaned and saw Keith standing there, there was no doubt that I had made the right decision. There was no competition. He was the man I was going to marry. I knew all the details would work out because he was the one I loved and wanted to spend my life with.

As soon as Keith and I left the airport, I decided to tell him the story about Mack. I just could not hold it in. His first response? "Those roses were worth a lot of money—you should have kept them. I wouldn't have minded it."

One day later, I drove to Minneapolis alone because I had an interview at a television shopping channel for an on-air position. It was a last-minute development arranged by Leesa, who had just landed an on-air job at the network. I decided that I should interview and see what would happen from there.

It was a rainy day, and Leesa was moving into her new apartment not far from the studio. The interview went fine, but I was not so sure that it was the job for me. I ran out to the car and threw open the door. As I was getting in, the door sprang back, and the metal corner hit me in the forehead. Immediately, I fell across the seat, holding my head in agony. I saw stars and was delirious. Here I was in Minneapolis alone in Keith's car, and I was injured. I looked at my forehead in the mirror; it was blown up with a huge black and blue knot. Tonight was the dress rehearsal for the wedding, and I was going to meet family members for the first time. Oh, great.

I remembered that Leesa's apartment was on this road somewhere near me, but I had never been there. I started driving until I saw an apartment complex with a big moving truck. This had to be her place. Sure enough, I walked in the entrance to find her and her mother standing there. That had to be God's work! They freaked out about my head and made me lie on a couch. After a while, they insisted on taking me to an urgent care center, where I was told that I had a slight concussion. I rested for a few hours, then I had to drive south ninety minutes to get to the farm. What a great start to the wedding weekend!

A little bit of makeup helped hide my bulging head. The wedding was beautiful, and somehow, I caught the bride's bouquet. That was a first for me. Keith was handsome, dressed in a tuxedo. Once the dancing was underway, I asked Keith to take me back to his uncle's house because my head was hurting. The concussion was a real party killer. When he took me to my room, I set my things down on a table and turned around. Keith was down on one knee.

"Lisa, I love you. Will you marry me and spend life with me?"

There was no debate. No doubt. I said, "Yes," even without a ring. My questions had all been answered, and I was ready for the rest of my life.

TAKEAWAYS FOR LIFE

Fear of the unknown keeps many of us from achieving our goals or from realizing our dreams. It is simply being afraid of what you do not know. We all experience this in one manner or another. For some, it simply manifests as anxiety about the future. We are worried about how situations are going to turn out or how we are going to overcome hurdles we are up against. But the Bible tells us that we need Faith over Fear.

What is faith? Hebrews 11:1, NIV, says, *"Now faith is confidence in what we hope for and assurance about what we do not see."* Or, as the Message Bible says, *"Our faith is the firm foundation under everything that makes life worth living. It's our handle on what we can't see."*

We cannot have hope without faith. When I realized I was falling in love with a man who lived 700 miles away on a pig farm, I had fears. This was not exactly how I had planned out my life. There was so much I could not control. I did not want to move. I did not want to leave my job or change careers. And I certainly did not want to live on a pig farm. I was walking in fear more than I was in faith. Fear can steal your joy, your peace of mind, and your hope for the future.

When I finally surrendered every area of my life and trusted God with all of my questions and doubts, I started overcoming my fears. Did that mean everything I was about to encounter was going to be easy? Not at all. It meant that I trusted God to walk with me in every situation. I knew that He had only the best in mind for me, and I was not alone in facing the future.

Once you have laid down your fears before Jesus, there will be temptation to pick them up again. We tend to run back to what we have left behind. We start second-guessing our decisions. That is why prayer is so important. When you are in constant fellowship with Jesus, He gives you the strength to leave your fears at the altar and simply follow Him. Remember that God is with you, and He is for you.

CHAPTER 3

IN THE REARVIEW MIRROR

After twelve dates over fourteen months, I made the biggest decision of my life. I said, "Yes!" Our October wedding was fast approaching, and, of course, there were the details that every girl dreams of. Although I was not the fairy tale type, I did know exactly what I wanted, and most of it was pretty simple. I rented my wedding dress for $100 and the bridesmaids' dresses for $75. The boutique had everything I liked, so why buy? Mom had a silk and dried flower business and was making the flower bouquets.

I wanted to plan my reception alone as any good television producer would. It was not the food I cared about (which, by the way, was a beef and noodle dinner made by Mom's church friends). I wanted my talented singing friends to share our favorite Christian songs in a well-produced program. A broadcaster friend was the Master of Ceremonies. His smooth radio voice pulled everything together. I figured this would be the last program I would produce in a while as I said goodbye to Ohio.

Letting go of something you really enjoy doing is difficult. I loved working in television and did not know whether I would get the opportunity again. My love for interviewing and writing all started when I was ten. Mom gave me a tape recorder for Christmas. I pretended to be legendary journalist, Barbara Walters, and interviewed family and friends everywhere I went. Maybe now something even better was just around the corner for me.

Falling in love with Keith changed everything. I surrendered my life plans fully to the Lord. According to the goals I had mapped out in college, I was supposed to be an accomplished writer by now. Instead, I was heading to a town in Minnesota where no one knew my name. I laughed, thinking about the lyrics to the theme song from the television show *Green Acres*. "Green Acres is the place to be; Farm livin' is the life for me..." Just like that, I was actress Eva Gabor, moving from the city to a pig farm.

Facing A New Life

I was moving away from everything and everyone I knew. Frankly, I barely knew Keith's family. I had met his four sisters a couple of times, but we really did not know each other. His father, George, was sweet and quiet. As I have mentioned, Keith's mother, Rosalyn, died of cancer at age fifty-two, just a couple of years before we had met. Keith had quit college and football after one year to help his dad run the farm. George spent much of his time helping Rosalyn, especially in her final months.

Breast cancer had struck when her youngest daughter, Carolyn, was a baby. The cancer progressed over the years, even with periods of remission. She continued to pray that she would live to see Carolyn graduate from high school. Keith and his sisters were forced to grow up fast during those years. The oldest girls took on the role of being a mother—cooking, cleaning, and helping their mom be as comfortable as possible.

After eighteen years of fighting the battle, Rosalyn died a few months after Carolyn graduated. But her prayer was answered. After Keith had told me this story on the cruise, I realized there was a lot of pain and loss that his family had gone through. Yet they were all strong people with a reverence for God and great love for each other.

I looked at photos of his mother as I was preparing for the wedding. I felt great sadness for all of them. I knew they would have loved for her to be here to see her only son get married.

My emotions were all over the place in those few days before the wedding. When your life is about to change drastically, your mind swirls with memories and the experiences that had impacted your life. For me, there were a few that stood out from the rest.

Getting Back Up

First, there were the Forrest Gump leg braces. When I was less than two months old, Mom noticed that my right leg kicked slower than my left. The doctor diagnosed me with a dislocated hip as a result of being born breech (feet first). In today's world, surgery would have probably corrected the problem. But in the 1960s, a series of leg braces was the answer. I started with an infant pillow brace that held my legs apart; then I advanced to a couple other braces when I started walking.

Before I knew it, I became pigeon-toed and now had full- length braces with rubber hoses attached to heavy, clumpy shoes. Everything was connected to a three-inch wide leather belt strapped around my waist. If you watched the legendary movie *Forrest Gump*, you can envision what I am talking about. I wore them all day and had to sleep in them at night. Yes, that included the clumpy shoes.

I was not handicapped, but some people looked at me that way. I learned that adults show sympathy and go out of their way to help you. They took pity on me and wanted to pick me up whenever I fell down, although Mom would never let them because she wanted me to be independent.

Children do not usually show the same sympathy as adults. Some made fun of me at school. They would run up to me during recess and kick my leg braces. Then they would run away and laugh. If I tripped and struggled to get up, they laughed even harder. This became a normal part of my school days. I do not remember yelling at them or crying over the way they were treating me. I was determined to keep playing and not let them get the best of me.

The taunting did not make me want to give up; it actually made me more determined. I believed that this was just a short phase in my life and there would come a day when I no longer had to wear the braces. Mom promised me that we would burn the braces in a bonfire when that day came. And we did when I was about ten years old. Several years later, she wrote me a birthday letter describing what she remembered about those early years.

> *No matter what you wore or endured, it never slowed you down. You were quite impish in your personality and feisty in your achievements; you basically haven't changed much. I wouldn't let anyone drown you in pity. No, you never were a wimp. You learned to sit up, crawl, and eventually walk and run, but it took a lot more determination on your part.*
>
> *There were lots of challenges, including the ugly high-top shoes built up to throw your feet out. You had to wear these because the braces made you pigeon-toed. I'll never forget when you finally could wear your first pair of tennis shoes! I guess this is why you hold a special place with me.*
>
> *Experiences such as this make for special bonding. Let me say that I did not do this on my own strength. Almost daily, I asked*

God for enough strength for the next day. As always, He came through.

Blindsided By Loss

In my teen years, other life events influenced who I became later in life. At age sixteen, my friend Beth was fun-loving with high energy. She was a cheerleader, class officer, a great student, and she loved to laugh. She and I were close friends, but Beth really was a friend to all. Both of us worked part-time at Burger King, and our dads worked at the Ford Motor Company.

The summer of 1976 held exciting promises for our upcoming junior year. When Beth came to my house, we always made memories. The last time I was with her, we belted out "I Did It My Way" at the top of our lungs as I pounded the piano keys.

It was August, and I was taking driver's education training at school. That particular morning, my friend Kathy walked into the classroom and sat next to me.

"I had a strange dream early this morning," Kathy said, almost in slow motion. "I dreamed that the radio station said that Beth and her dad had died in a house fire."

My eyes widened, and I immediately responded with, "Gosh, that's a really sick dream." But something inside of me shuddered. I felt goosebumps on my arms.

I watched as other classmates arrived. They were upset, sad, or crying. I refused to believe what Kathy said was true until Joey walked in the door.

He was sobbing and shaking. Joey lived next door to Beth. I now knew this horrible story was true. I felt nauseated and lay my head on my desk. I felt like someone had just kicked me in the stomach. Then the tears gushed. I could not even hear the teacher speaking. No one could. Why would something like this happen to such a wonderful family? Why did Beth and her dad have to die? The other four children and their mom were left all alone.

The days that followed were gut-wrenching for their family and our entire community. The house fire was caused by a faulty television in the basement where Beth and her older sister slept. There was only one tiny window in the basement, but Shelly somehow busted it, climbed out, and ran around the house to the front door. She frantically pounded with a bloody hand until the family woke up. Everyone but Beth was outside. Her father ran back into the house to rescue her. When he opened the door to the basement, the backdraft exploded. He and Beth were gone.

That was my first experience with death. The agony I felt could not compare to anything else I had ever gone through before. When I close my eyes now, forty-eight years later, I still see myself sobbing at the cemetery with my classmates. I can see the funeral cars pull away with the oldest sister screaming and crying out the window. She is stretching her arms toward her father and sister's gravesite.

I was devastated. I could not understand why this had happened. That was my earliest memory of asking God, "Why?" Why did they have to die? What hope does any of us have of living a long life? I found myself becoming withdrawn and bitter. I started writing dark, sad poems about life.

> *I found myself becoming withdrawn and bitter. I started writing dark, sad poems about life.*

I remember one poem talked about me feeling like a piece of debris floating in the ocean. I was tossed to and fro. It felt like I did not know where I was going to end up. I felt pretty hopeless, but God had better plans for me.

My parents had me go to church since I was a child. I knew Bible verses and stories, but I knew very little about a personal relationship with Jesus Christ. After losing Beth, I was looking for something to shake up my life and make it better.

I met a new friend who was two years older than me. She took an interest in me and started sharing her hope. I visited her church a few times and was surprised at how excited people were about worshiping God. This was so different from what I had experienced in the church I grew up in.

Accepting Jesus

Was I really ready to get serious with God? I still had so many questions about life and death. How did I know He would be for me and not against me? Deep inside, I knew I could not continue floating in the ocean with nowhere to go.

On New Year's Eve, I was babysitting. The kids were in bed, and the doorbell rang. I was shocked to see my new friend standing there. She was supposed to be at a church New Year's Eve party but decided to come see me instead. After getting mugs of hot chocolate, we sat on the couch, and she started talking.

"Lisa, we have talked for a while now about what it means to be a Christian. Jesus came to the earth to show us that He is the Way, the Truth, and the Life. No one comes to the Father God except through Jesus." Her eyes were intent on mine. "Jesus gave up His life for us—for you and for me. He died on the cross and sacrificed it all so we could have eternal life even after this one ends."

We talked in great detail about who Jesus was and why He would make a difference in my life right now. I knew the time was right for me to pray and ask Jesus Christ to be the Lord of my life. I had been running with no direction. I got down on my knees and asked him to forgive my sins and start leading my life.

I cried and cried and felt such a relief inside. I knew I would never be the same again. The peace and hope I had longed for was going to come from Jesus, not from anything else in the world. It was a great way to start the new year!

Time went by quickly, and before I knew it, I was a senior. I was growing in my faith and learning a lot about how the Bible applied to my everyday life. I realized that Christians were not exempt from the trials of life. What I did not know was that I was about to learn that firsthand.

I realized that Christians were not exempt from the trials of life. What I did not know was that I was about to learn that firsthand.

LISA KROEHLER

A Time To Weep

Mike was a couple of years older than me, and he was fun to be around. We hung out at post-game events and eventually tried dating. We realized pretty quickly that we were destined to remain friends. After a couple of months, I lost track of him. He did not call or show up at our usual hangouts. Then, through the grapevine, I heard that he was sick. I did not think much of it at first until I found out that he had a brain tumor and had surgery.

I knew it was pretty serious, and I needed to see him. But with high school graduation and everything that went with it, I did not attempt to see him until early June. I was really nervous about it because I did not know what to expect. When I walked into the house, I was shocked to see that he was partially paralyzed and lying on the couch. He could still talk but chose not to say much. His mother greeted me with a quiet smile, but I could see the pain in her eyes. This should not be happening to a twenty-year-old.

After that first visit, I committed to riding my bike to his house in the country a couple times a week. Each time, he was lying on the couch, staring at the ceiling. As the days went on, he spoke less and moved less.

I did most of the talking and had no problem doing it. I talked about everyday life. I wanted him to feel normal, although I knew that was impossible. Then one day, I decided it was time to talk about something that really mattered: eternal life. I started sharing about my faith in God and how I had come to the realization that I needed Jesus in my life.

I shared the scriptures that were very personal to me. I talked about heaven and the hope of eternal life. Mike never asked any questions, but sometimes he would shake his head, yes or no. His eyes said a lot. They darted back and forth, especially when I prayed.

My heart hurt badly for him as the prognosis was poor. He was not expected to live. I could not imagine everything going through his mind. He was constantly on my mind; it caused me to think about Beth, who had died two years before. What was I supposed to learn from all this? Based on what I knew about Beth, I believed that she was in heaven and I would see her again. As I watched Mike rapidly fading away, I felt deep compassion for him. I prayed he would find peace with God. I started spending more time sharing about the hope of heaven. I wanted him to know that there was a place where there was no more pain, no suffering, and no loneliness.

One time, he told me that he did not believe there was a heaven or hell. I told him that was a copout. You had to make a decision one way or the other.

"Let's say you're right and I am wrong," I told him. "If I believe in heaven when I die, and I find out there is not a heaven or hell, what difference would that make? But if I die not believing in anything at all, and there is a heaven and hell, then I have lost everything."

I prayed with him and for him many times. In my heart, I did believe that he gave his heart to Jesus before he passed away that summer. At the funeral, a lot of tears were shed by many young people. Losing another friend forever etched in my heart how precious and unpredictable life is. Age does not matter. This stirred my spirit to want to share Christ with others. I wanted to make a difference. People need people who care about them. But people really need the God who saves them.

NEVER SAY NEVER

TAKEAWAYS FOR LIFE

Sometimes, it is helpful to look in the rearview mirror—not only to remind us of how far we have come but also to show us how hard times can make us stronger. The death of my young friends made me want to become a light for those facing darkness. As a teen, I realized quickly that none of us are guaranteed a long life. As hard as it is to understand, it is the reality of life. We should make the most of every day, even when the days are difficult.

My walking problems for the first few years of my childhood taught me that I needed to get up every time I fell down. That did not mean that I got up quickly. In fact, does anyone ever jump up quickly when you have taken a hard fall? No. It takes time and effort. First, you lie there, thinking about what just happened. You realize that you have to get up even though there may be some pain involved.

That is the only way you can move on with your life. You roll onto your side and slowly get on your hands and knees. Then you crawl toward something sturdy to grab onto to help pull you up. I remember vividly that that had happened to me when I had severe COVID-19 in 2021. My body was weak, and I tried to walk to the garage. I collapsed face down on the mudroom tile floor. There was no one around to help me, and I had to stop moaning and make an effort to move.

I rolled over, got on all fours, and crawled to a sturdy bench. I used it to help pull me up. But I did not start walking right away. I sat on the bench for a few minutes, regained my composure, and then garnered the strength to stand.

May I ask you what you are grabbing onto to pull yourself up? What is your sturdy bench when you are down and discouraged? You have probably heard of the old hymn that says, "On Christ the Solid Rock I stand, all other ground is sinking sand. All other ground is sinking sand." Christ is the firm, unshakable foundation when everything else around us is unstable. I grab onto the rock that does not move. He is always there when I need Him. Even when I don't think I need Him, He is still there.

> *"The Lord is my rock, my fortress and my savior;*
> *My God is my rock, in whom I find protection. He is my shield, the power that saves me,*
> *And my place of safety."* Psalm 18:2, NLT

CHAPTER 4

GREEN ACRES – LIFE ON THE FARM*–

After a wonderful wedding and goodbyes to my family, we hit the road for Minnesota. The farmhouse where I once said, "I could never live here," was now my home. Keith had renovated the upstairs of the original house and turned it into a modern apartment with a separate entrance and sunroom.

His dad lived downstairs until he remarried a while later. The farm, Rosewood Farms, was originally owned by Keith's grandfather. At age nineteen, Keith bought the farm from the estate and continued operating the pig farm with his dad. The eleven-acre homestead included an original two-story house, an old detached garage, and two big barns. Keith's dad owned additional acres of land and woodlands around the farm.

Life on the farm

Before I met them, Keith and his dad were very capable bachelors who worked tirelessly raising and selling European Large White/Landrace breeding hogs. The days were long and dirty, and their wages were pretty meager for all they put into it.

At first, I kept busy, turning his bachelor pad into a home. After I finished decorating, I decided I needed to improve my cooking skills. After all, I had plenty of time and many recipe books received as wedding gifts. I even experimented with recipes from his family's cookbook. I learned quickly that pig farmers would not always be on time for dinner. Unexpected problems occurred with the pigs—or broken water pipes—or something else to delay him in the barns.

Many times, dinner sat there for two or three hours, waiting for him to come in after dark. Then, when he did sit down at the table, Keith loved pouring spices on his food before he even tried it. That was a newlywed pet peeve after having labored over my home cooking. But there were bigger fish to fry than worrying about the spices.

I started getting lonely after a few weeks. He was gone before I woke up and came in late most nights. I had no one to talk to. I did not have any friends and did not want to call Mom in Ohio every day. I needed to figure out my new life. The nearby town of Henderson was adjacent to the Minnesota River. There were no fast food restaurants, pizza delivery - or even any stop lights. The closest shopping mall or a Walmart was more than thirty miles away.

> *I started getting lonely after a few weeks. He was gone before I woke up and came in late most nights. I had no one to talk to.*

But Henderson had a quaint Main Street with a Hallmark feel. The town drugstore had an old-fashioned soda fountain; it was a good place to sit and get to know people. That's where I met the publisher of the town newspaper. He was happy to hear that I had a newspaper background since he was looking for a "volunteer" to write stories about the local residents. That was my first start in becoming a part of the town and the beginning of me finding out who I was in this new life.

Life changed pretty rapidly for me once I started meeting people. Not only the locals but also the media and Christian leaders in the Twin Cities. For a while, I was a freelance writer for a video production company and a nationwide ministry. Those connections led me to be hired as a field representative for the Pat Robertson presidential campaign.

I traveled to twenty-eight counties and organized meetings and turnouts for the upcoming Minnesota caucus. That led to me overseeing those same counties for a congressional and a gubernatorial campaign. After the caucuses were over, a wealthy Christian businessman who knew me from the presidential campaign hired me to be the managing editor of *People & Politics*. This was his new conservative political magazine, focusing on the upcoming 1988 election. I hired writers and photographers and worked with a graphic design company. It was exciting pursuing something I loved, but it required me to work a couple hours drive from the farm.

Keith and I decided to rent an apartment about halfway in between. We stayed at the apartment a few nights a week and lived on the farm on the weekends. It sounded way more glamorous than it was. When I hear about celebrity couples living apart in two cities, I know that it puts immense stress on the relationship. Our rendezvous did not always work out because of commitments he had on the farm or late-night deadlines I had in the Twin Cities.

It felt like our lives were drifting apart, yet I felt the pressure of maintaining my good income.

We were almost a million dollars in debt on the farm. I knew about this before we were married, but it did not really sink in until months later. A multi-generational farm is likely to have debt, especially with the high inflation of the 1970s. The financial burden was great on Keith and his dad. The stress started affecting Keith physically; he would roll on the floor in pain, moaning as he held his stomach. There just were not enough sales to cover the farming costs and the debt.

I felt helpless. If I quit my job, I knew that would put us in a worse financial situation. My decision to leave the Twin Cities pretty much was mapped out for me. The election magazine was published, and the future of it was unsure. We canceled our apartment lease, and I moved permanently back to the farm. The magazine retained me as a short- term consultant while the owner figured out its future. I made a part-time income and inherited a fax machine, so it was a pretty good gig out in the country.

They Are All Gone

By this time, I was twenty-eight, and Keith was thirty-two. We decided to start a family. It did not take long before I was pregnant. I had morning sickness all day! I could not even swallow my own saliva without getting sick. I wore a towel on my shoulder and looked ghostly. I had stopped working completely, which hurt our finances even more.

One morning, I was feeling exceptionally sorry for myself as I lay on the couch. My life had been turned upside down; it felt like our problems were closing in on us. I just wanted to call Mom and talk to her, but I did not want my parents to know how bad our situation was.

All of a sudden, Keith threw open the front door and was standing in the living room sobbing. "They're dead! They are ALL dead!" he yelled. I had no idea what he was talking about. At first, I was afraid that he had found his dad unconscious; then I realized he was talking about the 50 lb. feeder pigs that had just been delivered by a neighboring farmer the day before.

We had not even paid for the pigs yet! How could this happen? Keith tried telling me some of the details, but he was so distraught. Somehow, the methane gasses from the sewer pit under the floor rose up and asphyxiated the pigs. None of the 159 pigs had survived.

The next few hours were agonizing. Keith, his dad, and our pastor threw the pigs out of the barn into a high pile. It was a sad, disgusting sight. All I could think of was that our life on the farm was over. We would have to file for bankruptcy and walk away with nothing. I cried out to the Lord, begging him to help us. I believed in the power of prayer, and I knew that God cared about every detail of our lives. I also knew that sometimes His answers are not what we want to hear.

I was preparing myself for whatever was going to happen. I recalled the miracle we had had a few months ago when a $2,500 IRS check mysteriously showed up in our mailbox. It was dated a year earlier. Where did it come from, and why did it show up a year later? I believed that it was God's perfect timing. It also reminded me of God's faithfulness when we least expect it. We say that we believe. We pray and ask, but then we are surprised when He does a miracle and intervenes in our lives just in time.

"Lord, here I am again," I prayed out loud as I lay on the couch. "You see our mess. I don't know where we are going or what our purpose is. But I believe you know it and can lead and direct us."

I was reading my Bible, where Moses told the children of Israel that Joshua would lead them into Canaan, the promised land (Deuteronomy 31:6). "Be strong and courageous! Do not be afraid, and do not panic before them. For the LORD your God will personally go ahead of you. He will neither fail you nor abandon you."

I held onto that verse, knowing God was with us, regardless of our circumstances and the outcome. It was a long night, but as always, a new morning came. And this time, it came with a miracle. The farmer who owned the pigs was not holding us financially responsible. He was forgiving our debt!

There was such a spiritual lesson here. We did not deserve to be forgiven, and he did not owe us that. But he chose to forgive our debt, anyway. That is exactly what Jesus did when He died on the cross. He paid a debt He did not owe, and we owed a debt we could not pay. It was the ultimate sacrifice.

This farmer's great gesture of generosity helped us stay in business, although we knew changes were coming. We cherished this undeserved gift from God. No matter what was going to happen in our future, we knew He would not abandon us. We have never forgotten that miracle.

Facing The Truth

My uncle Terry was an evangelist; he came to stay with us a few days when he was holding tent revivals in the area. One morning, while in prayer, he saw a dark cloud and claw of poverty over our farm. We had not told him anything about our financial situation, but evidently, the Lord did. He prayed with us, asking the Lord to break the claw and lead us into financial freedom. Hearing about a claw of poverty over our farm led Keith to delve more into the spiritual implications of our struggles. Our pastor in the Twin Cities was a great counselor; we met with him to get his insights. Keith began telling his story.

"When I was eighteen years old, helping my dad on the farm, we had a lot of debt and a lack of cash flow. Dad was trying to get a loan to help with the building we had under construction, but he could not get one from the banks," Keith recalled. "Dad and I met with a farmer in a nearby town known for giving loans to farmers, but he turned down our request."

Several days later, Keith decided to return to the farmer alone and asked him again.

"I went back there under the pretense that I wanted to be a farmer, and he should help us save the family farm. I told him how much the loan would mean to us, and it would help the next generation. The farmer changed his mind and decided to give us the loan."

When Keith finished his story, the pastor looked up from taking notes and asked. "What did you mean by pretense? Did you really want to be a farmer?"

Keith looked down and thought for a moment. "I really didn't know then. I just said what I thought he wanted to hear because we were desperate."

"So, basically, you lied," the pastor said.

Keith looked startled, then tears welled up in his eyes. "An arrow just pierced my heart when you said that."

The pastor was a gentle man, but he did not mince words. "Your involvement in the farm was founded on a lie. You really wanted that farmer to think you were sold on becoming a farmer when you really had no idea what you wanted to do. God cannot honor decisions based on the foundation of a lie."

> *Keith looked startled, then tears welled up in his eyes. "An arrow just pierced my heart when you said that."*

Even though Keith was not responsible for the financial problems that had occurred before he was an adult, he became part of the ensuing darkness when he lied about his own future just to get the loan money. The pastor said he understood why a young man would want to help save his family's farm, even to the point of twisting his words to get the attention of the wealthy farmer. But the foundation was made of sand, and the Bible explains the results clearly.

Anyone who listens to my teaching and follows it is wise, like a person who builds a house on solid rock. Though the rain comes in torrents and the floodwaters rise and the winds beat against that house, it won't collapse because it is built on bedrock. But anyone who hears my teaching and doesn't obey it is foolish, like a person who builds a house on sand. When the rains and floods come and the winds beat against that house, it will collapse with a mighty crash. Matthew 7:24-27, NLT

The pastor prayed with us, and Keith asked the Lord to forgive him for what had happened in the past. Some people would say that we were over analyzing the situation; others would say he was off the hook of responsibility because he was so young. We both knew we needed to face the truth and the mistakes of the past for us to move on as a married couple. We were not sure what would happen next in our lives, but we knew that this encounter would make us stronger. We were a united front.

LISA KROEHLER

TAKEAWAYS FOR LIFE

How do we respond when we are confronted with the truth that hurts? None of us likes being put on the hot seat. Keith was taken off guard when the Pastor questioned him about the "pretense" that he wanted to be a farmer. He did not know at age eighteen if that was what he wanted for a career, but he told the wealthy farmer it was his plan so he would loan them the money.

I do not believe Keith wanted to trick the farmer, and I do not believe he thought he was lying. He was just trying to save the family farm, although it was not really his responsibility. The bottom line was that Keith's career as a farmer was started on a foundation of sand, not rock.

If we are honest, all of us, at one time or another, have avoided confronting the truth. Sometimes, avoiding the truth or sugarcoating it seems to help us initially, but eventually, it comes back to haunt us. That avoidance can have long-lasting consequences. I think back to Keith's encounter with truth and how he responded to it. First, he did not lash out at the messenger. It is so easy to strike back at someone who is pointing out the truth in our lives when we do not want to hear it.

Keith also did not deny the pastor's observations. He could have made a lot of excuses and debated with the pastor about why he did what he did. But instead, he let the pastor's words shine light on his past. Keith truly said,

"An arrow just pierced my heart," when the pastor confronted him with the truth.

This reminds me that our mistakes have to be acknowledged and exposed before any healing can take place. We can choose to stay in a place of indifference and make excuses for our actions. Or we can choose to accept the truth, even as hard as it is, and embrace a fresh start.

> *John 14:6, NIV, Jesus answered, "I am the way and the truth and the life. No one comes to the Father except through me."*

And for me, the following verse is the key to walking in the truth of Christ.

> *"A final word: Be strong in the Lord and in his mighty power. Put on all of God's armor so that you will be able to stand firm against all strategies of the devil. For we are not fighting against flesh and blood enemies, but against evil rulers and authorities of the unseen world, against mighty powers in this dark world, and against evil spirits in the heavenly places. Therefore, put on every piece of God's armor so you will be able to resist the enemy in the time of*

evil. Then after the battle you will still be standing firm. Stand your ground, putting on the belt of truth and the body armor of God's righteousness. For shoes, put on the peace that comes from the Good News so that you will be fully prepared. In addition to all of these, hold up the shield of faith to stop the fiery arrows of the devil. Put on salvation as your helmet, and take the sword of the Spirit, which is the word of God." Ephesians 6:10-17 NLT

CHAPTER 5

CHASING THE WIND

Entrepreneurs think outside of the box. Keith was intrigued by the unusual ventures he had read about, heard about, or dreamed about. As a farmer, his life so far had been mapped out. Although he went to college on a football scholarship, his family circumstances led him back home after one year. He was a hard worker who would not give up regardless of the struggles. He loved coming up with new ideas on the farm and implementing new time-saving methods. In his mind, though, he was always looking for something else—something new he could learn or develop. It was not just about money; it was about the challenge of the unknown. He was an entrepreneur at heart.

Eventually, the farm corporation went through bankruptcy. Keith's dad, the majority owner, took the biggest hit financially. Keith still owed a lot of money and had no idea how we would pay off the loans. While still working on the farm, Keith did a couple of side stints, including selling adult athletic clothing and kids' water toys at outdoor festivals.

He made some money, but it was a short-term success. Then he got his insurance license and sold term life policies in the evenings. He was not passionate about any of these ventures, and they were not very profitable.

I was busy being a mom and doing a few freelance video writing projects. Again, there was not much money in it, but it kept my creative mind sharp. I kept praying that the Lord would show us where our lives were heading. Our firstborn, Jessica Rose, was our pride and joy. She was just a few months old when our lives took a new turn. Keith stopped raising pigs, and his uncle's hog operation rented our barns. Keith did not really have a career plan, but for the first time in his life, he was interviewing for jobs.

He was hired to set up promotional booths in retail stores. This was not his first choice, but it did have freedom and commission possibilities. The downside was traveling five days a week throughout Iowa, Nebraska, and Minnesota. Every time he returned home for the weekend, he could see how much our daughter had physically changed. That is when he started praying for a job closer to home.

Window Cleaning Inspiration

One week, he was working in a town near Lincoln, Nebraska, when he noticed a window cleaner. With a mop and squeegee, the man quickly cleaned storefronts on Main Street. Over and over, Keith saw this man at downtown shops. Most of us would move on and not think anymore about it. But as usual, Keith's curiosity got the best of him.

"Hey, how did you ever get into window cleaning?" Keith asked the man, probably in his late twenties.

"Well, I am getting my master's degree at the university, and I need to make good money at a job that can be flexible." He continued cleaning windows while he talked. "A California friend gave me a training video, and I caught on pretty fast. I make good money, and it is repeat business."

The "repeat business" comment got Keith hooked. Unlike contractors who build houses or pour concrete, a window cleaner can keep busy cleaning the same windows several times a year because they keep getting dirty.

Before he even returned home, he called California and ordered the training video.

I will never forget the day he walked into the house and proudly told me, "I'm going to be a window cleaner." That definitely is not what a wife expects to hear. I didn't even know that people made a living from window cleaning. But again, Keith thought differently than most people I knew. His mind was always churning and processing information.

When the video arrived, he started training himself. Before long, he was cleaning house windows within an hour's drive of us. He picked up some storefronts and was excited when he landed a small hospital account. The biggest problem was that we lived in such a rural area, and there was a lot of distance between jobs. He liked what he was doing, but if this was going to work, there were a few things he needed to figure out.

Like many entrepreneurs, Keith sometimes had the shiny object syndrome. A new business idea would pop up that would distract him from his original objectives or intentions.

> *Like many entrepreneurs, Keith sometimes had the shiny object syndrome.*

In a conversation with a friend, he learned that an area man made a lot of money selling 1919 draft root beer at the Minnesota State Fair. This was a popular root beer in our area, and as the story goes, the man made enough money in ten days to set aside a hefty amount for their children's education. Because Keith had sold at festivals before, he loved the idea of traveling to a state fair and trying root beer sales.

No, he was not giving up on window cleaning but thought this idea might help retire some of our debt quickly. Ever since I had known him, Keith fondly talked about his family's involvement in food ventures when he was younger. There was his mom's cafe, The Dabbler, in Henderson that served homemade comfort food, and then the Kroehler popcorn wagon (a version of the modern-day food truck) that sold popcorn, peanuts, hotdogs, and ham sandwiches at local celebrations.

At first, the idea of hitting the road with a root beer stand sounded interesting, maybe even fun. After all, we only had one child to take with us. As a planner, I usually look at situations in black and white. But this time, I admittedly did not ask enough questions. I was preoccupied with my two-year-old and not feeling well. I knew in my gut that I was pregnant again. Right before we left town, I found out that I was pregnant, and now I had full-fledged morning sickness twenty-four hours a day. Did I mention that we were becoming carnies?

LISA KROEHLER

Carnies On The Road

Unfortunately, this venture meant that we had to take out a bank loan to buy a used pickup and camper top. Yes, we would sleep in the back of the truck for the next few weeks. Then, there was the refrigerated trailer that we needed to haul fifty-two kegs of root beer. The root beer came in sixteen-gallon kegs and, during the trip, would be kept cold with dry ice. After that, we would need access to electricity twenty-four hours a day.

Since it was already October, there were very few choices of festivals or fairs. My husband was making the decisions at this point, but I am not sure why I agreed to travel to the South Texas State Fair in Beaumont, Texas instead of trying a festival located thirty miles from my parents' house in Ohio. I was starting to question my sanity, knowing that it was a twenty-four-hour driving trip. Beaumont was eighty-five miles east of Houston. I guess it was go big or go home.

Jessica and I rode in the back of the camper all the way there. We were closed off from the cab, and there was no way to communicate with Keith. We girls lay on a bunk bed and played the Let's Go Fishing game for hours and hours. We did stay at a hotel one night but parked in a lot the rest of the time when Keith wanted to rest.

When we finally arrived in Beaumont, I was shocked at how rundown the fairgrounds were. I always thought that things were bigger and better in Texas, but this certainly fell short. In 1991, there was no internet, and it was almost impossible to investigate anything thoroughly. We really misjudged a few things. All they told us on the phone was they would have a few hundred thousand attendees. We discovered that was a little exaggerated. No one paid admission, which meant many people had no intention of spending much money. I had a pit in my stomach. This was probably a forewarning of what was yet to come.

On a bright note, our root beer stand was located next to a vendor from Minnesota. A retired couple was traveling the southern US fair and festival route, selling their homemade German sausages and brats. That went along great with our Minnesota 1919 draft root beer, which they were very familiar with. As we were unloading our truck and talking to the couple, we became totally distracted. I suddenly had a strange sense that something was wrong. Where was Jessica? As a mom, there is nothing worse than the panicked feeling of a missing child.

I frantically ran out into the main concourse and searched the faces of all the people passing by. I was yelling her name, and my heart was pounding in fear. I would never forgive myself if something happened to her. I am sure Keith was searching too, but I was in the forefront and ready to tackle anyone who had my child.

Out of nowhere, a group of gypsies appeared and were walking toward me. There must have been at least eight to ten women wearing brightly colored long skirts, head scarves, and beautiful necklaces. Then I saw her. Jessica was holding the hand of one of the women, and they were all actually smiling at me. I ran to her and scooped her into my arms.

"This is your daughter?" one woman asked. "We found her walking alone. We thought she may be yours as you were busy unloading things."

I couldn't thank them enough for bringing her to me. I felt like such an idiot for letting her wander off. As I kissed Jessica's forehead and stroked her beautiful hair, I whispered a prayer of thankfulness to God for protecting her.

Day one of the ten-day fair was already off to an exhausting start. "Lord, are we supposed to be here? How do we know if we are doing the right thing? I know we prayed about this trip, but did we really want to know what you thought? Or were we just asking for your blessing on what we were going to do anyway?" I really grappled with those questions as the days went on, and so did the struggles.

Early October was still pretty warm in south Texas. After a couple of days of sleeping in the back of the camper with no air conditioning, I mentally lost it. The bed was hard, the camper was small, and I was just miserable with my nausea. The fair smelled of grilled shrimp, crawfish, Cajun food (even fried alligator), and other foods, and it was putting me over the edge.

I tried helping Keith with the root beer sales as much as I could, but it was difficult. Why did we think we could occupy a two-year-old all day at a state fair? I was so worried that I would lose her again. Keith decided we needed to find an affordable motel where we could rest comfortably and get away from the noise of the fair. That definitely was not an expense we had planned on, but at this point, it was a necessity.

Treading Water

The Minnesota couple was very sweet and talked to Keith about traveling with them to Jacksonville, Florida next. I could not even listen to those conversations at this point. Root beer sales here were not that great. We only had one other product - root beer floats. Had we really thought through a business plan, we would have realized that we had to sell a lot of root beer to cover our expenses. We were not likely to net much of a profit. To help save money, I found a couple of churches that offered free evening meals.

I never thought I would ever need to count on that, but sometimes you do what you need to do. It was humbling. We also learned that many people are generous and compassionate, and in South Texas, grits replace mashed potatoes. But root beer is not what they want at their state fair. Jacksonville, Florida was our next stop in this grand adventure. Obviously, I was reluctant but knew we had to keep going to recoup our expenses. There were no tears in leaving the fairgrounds in Beaumont, though.

Now we were on Interstate 10 in Louisiana on the longest bridge I had ever been on. The Louisiana Airborne Memorial Bridge (formerly the Atchafalaya Basin Bridge) runs between Baton Rouge and Lafayette. The eighteen-mile bridge is the third longest bridge in the US. Jessica and I sat up in the cab with Keith for this part of the trip. I was feeling fairly good, enjoying the views and conversation after such a stressful time in Beaumont.

Suddenly, the truck started knocking and riding rough. The check engine light came on. There was excessive white smoke pouring from the hood, and our engine power was decreasing. I could sense Keith's major anxiety as he knew this was something serious. We were pulling a big trailer full of root beer kegs. Thankfully, an exit was close by, and we limped into a Walmart parking lot.

Jessica and I sat in the overheated truck on that very hot Sunday afternoon while Keith paced outside, trying to figure out what to do.

"I think we blew a head gasket or something like that," Keith muttered. "I have to get on my bike and see if I can find a repair shop somewhere."

I moaned, "I doubt if anyone will be at a shop on a Sunday. Wow, what are we going to do—and it is so hot here."

Now Louisiana was on my list of states not to visit again. I don't think Keith even heard me; he was already getting the bike out of the trailer. He was on a mission and took off before I even had time to say anything. Jessica and I got out of the truck and went into the back camper. We played with some toys, but that did not last long because of the heat.

Back in the truck, Jessica played with the steering wheel. I was a mess. I looked out the window, hoping Jessica would not see me crying. What were we doing wrong? Why was this happening to us? This was just one more nail in our coffin. How would we even pay for repairs to this truck, and how long would it take? We could not stay in a camper in the Walmart parking lot. And I couldn't take the heat anymore. My nausea started up again. I'm sure it was triggered by stress. I finally did what I needed to do: I started praying, asking for divine intervention.

"Lord, I know you see the bigger picture. I can't see it, but you hold us in the palm of your hand because we are yours. Please, please let us find help." I begged the Lord. "And forgive us for any wrongdoings on our part. We cannot fix this mess without you. Only you can rescue us."

Rescued In The Bayou State

My crying turned to sniffles; I felt better after my prayer of surrender. This was when faith and hope had to kick in. Keith rode up on his bike, and he seemed calmer.

"I found a small auto repair shop; the owner was standing outside even though they were closed. He said he can help us but not until tomorrow. It may take a couple of days to fix it. But the crazy part is that he is a pastor of a church here. He is coming to pick us up and take us to a motel down the road."

I should not have been surprised that a pastor was rescuing us. I had no doubt this was the answer to our prayers. Before long, we were throwing our bags into his car and heading to a nearby motel. Even though they had a Walmart here, this was a fairly small town. It had just what we needed. We were thankful for this man's kindness and for a clean motel.

The pastor was probably in his fifties and had a southern drawl. His face beamed as he told us a little about the town and the church. When he dropped us off and made sure we had a room, he told us his wife was going to stop by later and bring us some food. And she did. Darlene was a beautiful, charming woman who seemed very genuine. Not only did we enjoy the homemade meal, but she told me she would like to pick us girls up tomorrow to stay at their house for the day.

Keith would be at the repair shop with her husband. She knew I was pregnant and would enjoy being in a home again. So, for two days, we spent a lot of time in this couple's small, beautiful home. She went out of her way not only to wash our clothes, but she played with Jessica so I could relax on their sofa and read a book. Not only did Darlene cook for all of us, but she even managed to get some white potatoes to replace the grits.

"I know how you Northerners like your mashed potatoes!" she said as she smiled sweetly.

They insisted we stay all night one night as the men were working late on the truck. Jesus was in their home. He was in every room and every conversation. I felt so peaceful in the middle of the storm that we were going through. While I was there, I did not think about money or how we were going to pay for the repair bill. I even stopped thinking about what was next on our journey. Darlene and I talked about the goodness of God and how He knows what we need and when we need it.

"The Lord has always showed up for us in all of our years together," she said. "We may not always like His answers or His timing, but God cares about every detail in our life, and He will always be with us. We have nothing without Him."

That resonated with me. There were many times in my life when I stressed over things I could not change. But God was there. Philippians 4:6-7, NLT says, *"Don't worry about anything; instead, pray about everything. Tell God what you need, and thank Him for all He has done. Then you will experience God's peace, which exceeds anything we can understand. His peace will guard your hearts and minds as you live in Christ Jesus."*

When the truck was finished, we hugged this amazing couple and thanked them for taking care of us. Keith told me later that Pastor Dan would only let him pay for the replacement parts, and he donated the labor costs. That was another miracle for us; we again said we would pass on those blessings to other people. Keith told me that he felt he was supposed to drive us north to Atlanta now and rent a car for Jessica and me. He wanted us to head to my parents' house in Ohio, where we could be comfortable and safe.

"I take full responsibility for the mess we are in," Keith admitted. "I don't know what I was thinking when I came up with this plan, but obviously, I missed a lot of the details. But because we have all of this added short-term debt now, I need to try to get rid of this root beer in Florida at a couple of shows."

I knew he was struggling as the head of the household. He was not a man of many words, but he more than once apologized for taking us on this trip. I reminded him that I agreed to do it; it was not like I was being held hostage. I did not want him to beat himself up over mistakes and poor decisions.

We said our goodbyes in Atlanta and headed north without Keith. He was going to catch up with the Minnesota couple in Jacksonville. I had a feeling that the Lord was going to use this time to speak a lot of things to him. For him, this was just the beginning of what was to come.

LISA KROEHLER

TAKEAWAYS FOR LIFE

I believe in angels. There has been more than one time in my life when someone showed up and helped me when I needed it. The first time was when a friend and I were traveling on a highway and saw an old man holding a sign by the side of the road. My friend, a pastor's daughter, prayed out loud, asking God if we were to pick him up since we were going to the same city. We ended up turning around at an exit and driving back to get the man.

I must admit that I was a little reluctant at first, but I changed my mind as the old man humbly talked about his love for Jesus and stressed over and over to us that God had a plan for our lives. There was something different about him, and I was greatly impacted by the words of faith he shared. When we dropped him off at a city street corner, we turned the corner in our car, and the old man was gone. There were no stores he could have walked into, no doors, nothing. He just quickly disappeared. My friend and I firmly believe this man was an angel sent to give us a word from God. I still believe that.

Fast forward to Louisiana in 1991. I still recall sitting in that Walmart parking lot on a sweltering hot Sunday. I cried and asked the Lord to help us, and He did. The pastor and his wife had offered us kindness, provisions, and even comfort in their own home. They may have been human, but they reached out to us like angels.

As Christians, we often talk about being the hands and feet of Jesus. But I look at my life and wonder sometimes how much I am really like that. Do I offer more than just money to someone to help them in their time of need? Am I likely to sacrifice something personal or even risk being uncomfortable to be an angel to someone else? This hits hard as I write this and remember how much that couple's unconditional kindness changed me at that time in my life. I felt rescued. Maybe He wants to use you and me to answer the prayers of others. I am open to that, are you?

"Trust in God" song by Elevation Worship (songwriters: Brandon Lake/Christopher Joel Brown/Mitch Wong/Steven Furtick)

> I trust in God, my Savior
> The One who will never fail
> He will never fail
> I trust in God, my Savior
> The one who will never fail,
> > He will never fail
> He didn't' fail you then, He
> > won't fail you now

LISA KROEHLER

I sought the Lord and He heard
    and He answered
I sought the Lord and He heard
    and He answered
I sought the Lord and He heard
    and He answered
That's why I trust Him, that's
    why I trust Him.

CHAPTER 6

FAILURE – PART OF THE FORMULA

As we all know, life doesn't always turn out the way we hope or plan. The Jacksonville festival was scrapped by Keith and the Minnesota couple because food was selling too cheaply. With their costs, they knew it would be another losing venture even before they started. They planned to meet up again in Hollywood, Florida, but that event did not start for three weeks.

Keith parked his truck, camper, and trailer at a campground on Daytona Beach. It was a shabby campground at best. Do you remember handsome James Garner playing Jim Rockford in the 1970s television show *Rockford Files*? He was a private investigator living in a rundown trailer on a beach. That is how I had envisioned Keith at this point. But instead of investigating criminal cases, he was investigating his own life.

What was he trying to prove in this business venture? Was it really the right decision to keep going to more festivals, hoping to turn this mess around? Yes, he had a beautiful view of the ocean in between gigs, but most everything else in his world right now was gray and cloudy. He was broke and had been living on root beer and sausages for a while. Meanwhile, Jessica and I were taking refuge at my parents' house in Ohio. I was trying to avoid conversations with my family about what Keith was doing in Florida.

Finding Their Way

Isn't it just like God to send someone into your life when you really need them? Keith met a Christian man named Barkley who also was on the festival circuit. He was probably in his late forties and understood Keith's penchant for entrepreneurial ventures. Barkley was pedaling a new type of ice cream called Dippin' Dots. They were flash-frozen beaded ice cream treats invented by someone Barkley knew. Keith and Barkley had a couple of things in common. They both were Christians, figuring out their life path and, in the meantime, worrying about keeping their festival products cold. Dippin' Dots had to be stored at negative 40 degrees Fahrenheit, and Keith had to make sure our root beer refrigeration kept working.

These two guys were adventurers at heart. They both wanted to be pioneers who made a difference in their worlds and their families. With a strong faith in God and a desire to follow Him, their discussions asked the hard questions. When the walls seem to be crumbling around you, does that mean you are out of God's will, or are you just facing mountains you have to climb? Are you crazy to think outside the box and try something risky when everyone else you know is playing it safe? Why is succeeding so difficult, but failing is so easy?

> *When the walls seem to be crumbling around you, does that mean you are out of God's will, or are you just facing mountains you have to climb?*

Neither of them had the answers, but just asking the questions was a good start to figuring out what was next for both of them. Keith's carnie idea had potential and had worked for others. But it was obvious there was more to it than he had planned. Instead of shaving off some short-term debt, he actually added to it. That weighed on him heavily, and he was feeling like a failure. It was a "Come to Jesus" moment for Keith. Alone in a camper with no money and no direction for his future, he prayed to the Lord, who cares about every detail of our lives.

"Lord, I know you are bigger than any mess we get ourselves into," he prayed. "Please help me and forgive me. I need you to direct my path instead of me always trying to do things my way. Please show me your way."

No Place Like Home

Meanwhile, my parents drove me back to Minnesota. It was almost Thanksgiving, which meant snowy weather was coming. In fact, twenty-nine inches had already fallen on Halloween. During the eleven-hour trip, my parents never brought up the subject of what was going to happen when Keith finally came home. They knew we were in heavy debt, but my parents firmly believed in letting their kids figure out their own problems. They never interfered or criticized. Of course, they would help you however they could, but paying off our debt was not their responsibility. With six children, they probably had plenty of practice in terms of self-restraint.

On Thanksgiving Day, Keith and Barkley ate a cheap turkey dinner at a Denny's Restaurant. Keith had never missed a family Thanksgiving before and was sad that Jessica and I were at his family's gathering without him.

I will never forget his phone call that day from a pay phone.

"I miss you and Jessica so much," he said in a trembling voice. I could tell that he was feeling down.

"I miss you more than you can know," I told him. "I know this has also been really hard on you. But I just have to know, when are you coming home?"

"I'm taking my last $75 and buying a bus ticket home. The truck broke down again. A farmer is letting me store the trailer at his orange grove, and a friend of his is storing the root beer kegs in a cooler."

The more he talked, the stronger his voice became. It was as if the decisions he had made helped him gain momentum. His voice was now more decisive, and he was sounding like the strong man I knew.

"It will take many hours on the bus to get there. I'll have to be picked up in the middle of the night." Then he was silent for a few moments.

"Lisa, I'm so sorry for what I have done to you and for the mistakes I have made. I am not giving up. I am committed to moving ahead and making something of our lives. I don't have it all figured out, but I do know that with God's help, we can turn things around."

LISA KROEHLER

Life Rolls On

On December 1st, Keith returned home in the middle of the night. As a gentle snow was falling outside, we stood in the living room and quietly embraced. There were no words to say right then, but the tears told it all. Despite the circumstances and the failures, we knew that we had only just begun to live.

Immediately, Keith took a job in a corporate chicken barn, where there were 100,000 caged chickens in each football field-sized barn. He quickly became a supervisor when he found ways to increase efficiency and productivity. Having been self-employed his entire life, setting production records was in his DNA. Keith was willing to do anything to help our finances, even if it meant working in animal barns again.

Keith was willing to do anything to help our finances, even if it meant working in animal barns again.

By this time, I was several months pregnant, and we did not have any insurance to help with maternity costs. Entering the welfare office was one of the most humbling things I have ever done. I weighed my options and knew it was something I had to do. I believed that medical assistance was designed to help people going through difficult financial times but was not designed to live on for the rest of their lives. We definitely qualified for it, and I had to swallow my pride to even take it short-term. After the baby was born, we discontinued it.

We named our son Joshua since we believed his birth was going to lead us into the promised land and help forge a new life for us. The Bible tells us that after the death of Moses, God called on Joshua to lead the Israelites across the Jordan River and take possession of the promised land. I love the characteristics of Joshua—he was courageous, a leader, a man of faith, someone who not only trusted in the Lord but who was obedient to Him. That was what we prayed for in our son.

Keith was able to sell some of the leftover root beer equipment he had left in Florida, and we recouped some of our money. That led to a serious discussion about our future.

"I am going to pay back every penny that the Kroehler name has ever owed," he asserted.

I was stunned.

"Why would you say that? You did not own even half of the farm operation, and some of that bank debt was never yours. It occurred before you were even an adult," I pointed out with much fervor. "It only seems right that you pay back your percentage of ownership, and that is all you are obligated to. Otherwise, we will be tied up for years and unable to move ahead. And just because of pride."

Those were stinging words to him at first. But as we talked more about our obligation, it became apparent that we should pay our share but not saddle ourselves with a debt we did not legally owe. Keith met with the banker and told him our intentions. Getting those affairs in order gave us a glimpse of hope that we could have financial freedom at some point.

Making that decision energized Keith, and he started thinking about starting a window cleaning business again. To my surprise, he wanted to move to my home city in Ohio, where the climate was a little milder. I had been in Minnesota six years and loved the idea of moving near my family.

Our barns were already rented, and the house had an upcoming tenant which would give us income to pay the farm mortgage. Two pig farmers bought items we had for sale, and that paid off the rest of the carnie loan. This was the most encouraged we had felt in a long time.

We were going to start over in Buckeye land with only $500 in our pockets and an old Ford Tempo. We had our little family and hope in our hearts.

NEVER SAY NEVER

TAKEAWAYS FOR LIFE

When we face failure, it is easy to feel like we will never make a comeback again. That is only true if we stay defeated and never rise up with resilience. Everyone has failures because the human race is flawed. No one is perfect, and despite our arrogance at times, we do not know everything. Life is about learning, and learning takes time, effort, and failure. It takes getting back up when you have been knocked down. It takes admitting you are wrong and need a different perspective. It takes commitment, discipline, and perseverance when the times get tough.

Baseball great Babe Ruth once said, "Don't let the fear of striking out get in your way." Success does not usually happen overnight. It can take a lot of strikes before you get even one hit. As you know, some of the greatest business people and inventors thrived despite their failures. In fact, they thrived because of their failed attempts. You have heard of them before: Walt Disney, Thomas Edison, Henry Ford, William and Orville Wright, Albert Einstein, and the list goes on.

> *"Don't let the fear of striking out get in your way." - Babe Ruth*

Failure drove them to re-evaluate their processes, reflect on what went wrong, and then they started over. Most successful entrepreneurs I know failed more than once before they succeeded in a business. That is because there is so much to learn from failure. If we got everything right the first time around, how would we learn to be overcomers? It is the same in our personal lives. The poor decisions we make can be used to turn our lives around in the right direction. Our egos get knocked down; we see our flaws and our need for a Savior. I know that when I am weak, He makes me strong.

Think about the many well-known people in the Bible who failed. Jonah refused to do what the Lord told him to do and ran away. He ended up on a ship and was thrown into the sea and swallowed by a whale. Finally, he saw the light, repented, and went to Nineveh as God told him to. King David had an affair with a married woman named Bathsheba, and she got pregnant. He even had her husband killed. Eventually, David repented and turned back to God. From him, we have the beautiful book of Psalms, and the Bible says he was a man after God's own heart.

Then I think of Simon Peter. He promised Jesus that He would always stand by Him. But the night Jesus was taken out of the Garden of Gethsemane, Peter denied that he ever knew Jesus three different times. Can you imagine how guilty and defeated he felt after he heard the rooster crow on his third denial? The Bible says he broke down and cried. But Peter repented for his failures, embraced the call God had on his life, and went on to preach the Gospel to thousands.

Failure teaches us valuable lessons and helps transform us into the persons we really want to become. Experiencing hardship and defeat hurts, but God uses our struggles to bring us closer to Him. It is usually through our failures and trials that we realize our great need for the Lord.

> *"Consider it pure joy, my brothers and sisters, whenever you face trials of many kinds, because you know that the testing of your faith produces perseverance. Let perseverance finish its work so that you may be mature and complete, not lacking anything."* James 1:2-4, NLT

> *"Trust in the Lord with all your heart; Do not depend on your own understanding. Seek His will in all you do, and He will show you which path to take."* Prov. 3:5-6, NLT

CHAPTER 7

TAKE TWO: STARTING OVER

Sharing an 1,100 square foot ranch house with my parents was not the ideal moving plan. Sometimes, starting over literally means from scratch. Fortunately, we only stayed with them for a few weeks before we found a rental house in the country.

The Zion Church Road two-story farmhouse was built in 1907. That certainly sums up its condition. The first time we walked inside, hundreds of dead flies were lying all over the upstairs carpet where the empty bedrooms were. I took a deep breath as I remembered our nicely remodeled farmhouse in Minnesota.

Our lives had been turned upside down these last couple of years, and it was our decision to move. Sometimes, you don't realize that starting over in your "promised land" is not going to be easy. I stood in the old house that day and told myself, "I can handle this." I knew I had to accept all of the challenges that would be set before me, just as I had over the last several years. But living here would be a big one.

"I know this house is not the most ideal place," Keith said, looking around the rooms. "But we can get it cleaned up and make it work for a while. I think we will probably only be here for about a year or so."

We actually ended up living there for six years. Never say never. There were much worse problems than dead flies after we moved in. Quarter-sized black spiders were everywhere, especially in the kitchen. Every time we moved something off the kitchen counter or in the laundry room, a black spider was guaranteed to run out.

My Worst Fears

My worst fear became reality every day in this house. Mice lived in the walls. We could hear them every night and would find them in our mouse traps almost every morning. I would lie in

My worst fear became reality every day in this house. Mice lived in the walls.

bed at night with a blanket over my head to protect my face. And yes, there were a couple of times when I swear a mouse ran across the top of my hair while I was in bed. To this day, I am very afraid of mice and actually disgusted by them.

After moving into the house, Keith was offered a job at a local moving company. They moved heavy industrial equipment. He made $5.50 an hour at the job, which was just $1.25 above minimum wage. It was great to get us started, but we both knew he was destined for much more. On his days off, he focused on acquiring more window cleaning accounts, which brought in more money than his moving job. Because there was another longtime window cleaning company in our city, Keith had to drive farther away to look for commercial work.

Just like in most sales, it took a lot of "no" answers before he got the one "yes," and it usually was a fast food restaurant. There were only so many restaurants you could clean by eleven a.m., which was the requirement of most places. Keith, admittedly, was not a cold-calling salesman. Sometimes, he found himself sitting in the parking lot of a business for a long time before he could talk himself into going inside to see if they needed a window cleaner. Anyone who has been in sales knows the sick feeling you get when you are repeatedly rejected. But you do what you have to do if you want to succeed.

It took many months before Keith had enough window cleaning accounts to cover a full-time job. That is when he left the moving company. Sometimes, people get over zealous and quit a job too early to pursue their new venture. We learned from past mistakes that it's better to hold onto both jobs as long as you can. One of his window cleaning routes was in Bellefontaine, where he cleaned windows every Wednesday. He had restaurants, a public library, and many other retail accounts, including a pizza restaurant. Keith asked management if he could clean windows AFTER their busy lunch pizza buffet with an ulterior motive in mind. There was always leftover pizza that they would throw away. The manager liked Keith and willingly let him take it home every week. For years, our kids knew Wednesday night was pizza night, but they didn't realize it was really God's gift to our budget!

For the first few months after moving to Ohio, I was home full-time with Jessica and Joshua. I tapped into my marketing skills and helped Keith break into the residential market in our area. I targeted higher-income residential houses with a letter and family photo. The personalized letter talked about him, a former farmer and a dedicated family man with a strong work ethic. Trust, honesty, and professionalism were important to people considering letting someone into their house to clean windows.

That was long before companies routinely did background checks on service people. Keith's goal was to elevate the profession of window cleaning and offer superior service beyond that of our competitors. The letter garnered many new clients over the next couple of years and was the beginning of developing long-term clientele and a reputation as the premier window cleaning company in our area. Keith was underway in this new profession.

Before long, I was hired as a part-time features producer for a daily magazine show at the Christian television station where I had previously worked. I loved the ministry show, but I knew a change was coming for me. The television station planned to start a ten p.m. weekday newscast and asked me to be the News Director and co-anchor. This was something I had always dreamed about but had never done to this extent. I finally felt like my newspaper and magazine background was merging with my television experience to create a dream role for me.

I hired reporters and videographers and worked with directors to plan the elements of daily news, sports, and weather. We strategized constantly how to succeed against an NBC affiliate that had ruled the market forever. Both Keith and I were excited about our new ventures but were wondering how we were going to juggle it all. I was supposed to work from 2 p.m.-11 p.m. (which realistically became 1 p.m.-1 a.m.), and he would work 5 a.m. to 4 p.m., so the children would only have to be at a babysitter's for a couple hours a day. Needless to say, our lives quickly became very hectic.

Nightly News Woes

Keith was a superhero dad. He had Jessica and Joshua all evening and put them to bed at night after long days of window cleaning. He never complained. He took them to the library every week, made play dough, and taught them how to make candles in buckets of water, and explored the countryside. He would bring me dinner in the newsroom a couple nights a week. From the outside, it appeared that we had it all together, but inside, I knew that never seeing your husband was a recipe for disaster.

From the outside, it appeared that we had it all together, but inside, I knew that never seeing your husband was a recipe for disaster.

There were also many work challenges. A Christian television station producing a local newscast confused people. I remember a woman calling and asking me not to run a story about her daughter, who was in serious trouble with the law.

"I know you understand how devastating that could be for our family, and since you're a Christian, I would expect you could just skip that story even if the other station is airing it."

Of course, I had to explain to her that I had to select stories based on news worthiness and not on someone's faith. She was so upset with my explanation that she accused me of not being a Christian at all. That type of problem surfaced a few times as people had different expectations of us than the networks. We not only covered daily news, but we also included positive community stories, regardless of someone's faith. Our other ministry programs centered on faith. It felt like we were always up against a wall.

There was only one other married person in the newsroom, and it was our sports director/co-anchor. His wife was a stay-at-home mother of one, and even though he worked nights, it appeared they had a more stable life than we did. All the other reporters and editors were single, and I felt they could not relate to the stress I was feeling. Then the unexpected happened.

"I am pregnant," I told the Station Director. "I plan to keep on working, though, so no worries," I assured him.

But I did not feel very assured, especially because I was sick as always during my pregnancies. Every night right before going "live" at ten p.m. I would run to the bathroom and throw up. I would touch up my makeup, run into the studio, and smile at the camera. After I had read the news and the sports anchor was on camera, I would run out of the studio and get sick again. I could hear the director in my ear piece saying, "And there she goes again."

The first four months were brutal. Then there was the eventual weight gain. On television, you already gain ten pounds from the cameras. I always seemed to gain forty pounds with every pregnancy just like my mom did with all six of hers.

Justin David Kroehler was born April 26, 1995; he was one month early. I had pre-eclampsia at the 8th month mark, and they induced me. He was only 5 lbs. 2 oz. and very fussy for the entire first year. His digestive system was not fully developed, and he always had trouble eating. I had eight weeks maternity/vacation leave and enjoyed every minute of being home with all three children.

I thought a lot about our lives but was convinced that we needed the money I made (which was not a lot at a Christian ministry). When I returned to work, nothing was the same. I was wrestling with the direction I should take, especially when I would lie down just after midnight, and Justin would scream and cry. I was exhausted, and morning always came early with a three-year-old and a six-year-old jumping on me by 6:30 a.m. It's pretty difficult to look great on television when you feel like you have been run over by a train.

I felt guilty about everything I did or did not do. How could I continue juggling all of these balls? I felt like a lousy mother and wife who was not doing anything well, including being a news director. But how could we financially make it without my income as Keith was still building his business?

Time for introspection

One day, I was picking my children up at my sister's house. She told me she was getting a divorce. I was shocked. I had no idea that there were problems. Then I started looking at my own life and how little Keith and I saw each other. The children were well taken care of, but we were not. This was a game-changer for me.

Shortly after that, Keith and I went out to dinner alone. I told him I wanted to quit my job.

"What? You've always dreamed of doing what you are doing. How can you give that up?" He was bewildered.

"I can give it up because I think it's what I am supposed to do. I am not home enough, and so much has been put on you. The kids need more of me than I can give. I believe I can help with the window business and write training videos on the side. We can make it financially and have a better life," I convincingly shared.

By Christmas that year, I was done with news and on a daytime schedule with the kids. I remember thinking that it was the best holiday season I could remember in a long time. This was totally my decision, based on what I believed needed to happen in our family. Everyone has to decide what is best for them. We had an actual plan to expand his business. I was hired for some writing projects and taught a part-time speech writing class at a local college. I had more time with the kids and was home at night when Keith was. By the kickoff of the spring window cleaning season, I was fully focused on picking up new commercial and residential clients.

My entrepreneur husband was thinking outside of the box again. In 1996, he and I produced two VHS videos (for homeowners and restaurants) teaching people how to professionally clean their windows. This was for a nationwide audience. We called the videos "I DO WINDOWS!" as a play on words for all the maid services that say, "I DON'T DO WINDOWS." (That is what IDW stands for today in our business logo).

We sold our videos at the National Restaurant Association trade show in Chicago along with start-up window cleaning equipment. Pizza Today Magazine wrote an article about us, which led to sales to several restaurant chains. After that, I sent out press releases to radio stations on the East Coast, talking about how a former pig farmer and television producer had teamed up to start a window cleaning business. I was booked on radio shows and bantered with DJs about spring cleaning tips while my kids were in the next room, watching Sesame Street. We still have a 1-800 phone number from twenty-eight years ago.

The internet was fairly new to the public, but we were determined to sell our products online. At that time, we had to enlist the help of a local college tech department to come to the house and get us on dial-up internet and set up our website. The tech said we were one of the first businesses in our city to get on the World Wide Web! My small home office was piled up with VHS videos, window cleaning equipment, and toys. I loved it! I was scheduling and billing customers, but I was in control of my time. Life was so much better.

After about a year, our business clientele was growing, and we hired our first field technician. Keith took Shaun under his wing, teaching him not only about window cleaning but also about life. He ended up working with us for eighteen years and often said that Keith was a great mentor.

At this point, running the business required more time, and selling videos was less important. It was obvious that the real money was in doing the window cleaning work, so I focused more on marketing. Keith, Shaun, and my younger brother, Jason, were cleaning windows, which meant collecting cash from some clients.

Keith's current system was stuffing cash into empty Burger King bags. Oh, how things change. Just like in life, there are seasons in a business. We were fledgling and figuring out everything from trial and error. The first edition of QuickBooks was released in the late nineties, and it became our accounting software. I really had no idea what I was doing but was determined to figure it out.

Every morning at seven a.m., window cleaners parked in our yard. My laundry room was the first meeting room, where they would get their schedules and take clean window cleaning towels out of our dryer. At the end of the day, they would put their dirty towels in my washer. This is how many small businesses start: a little start-up capital, no bells or whistles, just hard work and a dream.

We were tracking recurring accounts manually because there were no home service CRMs to do it for you. I had hand-written job lists for our window cleaners every day.

Surprisingly, the business was growing enough that we were able to start saving to buy a one-acre wooded lot in a subdivision where we wanted to build. That in itself was a miracle because, for years, we had been sending $1,000 a month to Minnesota to pay past farm debt.

This is how many small businesses start: a little start-up capital, no bells or whistles, just hard work and a dream.

Out of the blue, one day our banker called and proposed we give our farm back to the bank in exchange for wiping our slate clean. We had lost our tenants and just wanted to move on with our lives in Ohio. The chains were finally broken, and we were celebrating. The Lord had walked with us through it all, and we were grateful. But let me be clear: we had to do our part in all of this. It was difficult sending that money monthly, but it was our obligation. Now that chapter was coming to a close, and this was the beginning of a new dawn for us.

LISA KROEHLER

TAKEAWAYS FOR LIFE

Nothing in life is ever wasted. Everything we go through, good or bad, molds and shapes us into better people, that is, if we allow it. You have probably heard the saying, "Become better or bitter." When life trips us up, it's our choice as to how we face it. None of us are perfect, and sometimes we get stubborn and defensive or maybe even throw our fist at God because we want someone to blame. No one is exempt from having challenges. Thankfully, the Lord sees all that we go through and is willing to walk with us.

> Isaiah 43:19, NLT says, *For I am about to do something new. See, I have already begun! Do you not see it? I will make a pathway through the wilderness.*

Sometimes, we just need a fresh start. Fresh starts do not fix everything immediately, but with hard work and perseverance, we can find joy and hope again. That usually requires embracing change and believing that with God, all things are possible.

There are seasons of life that we all go through. After Mom died, I saw that she had her Bible bookmarked to

Ecclesiastes 3, where it talks about those seasons. There is a lot to ponder here.

> **A Time for Everything**
>
> *For everything there is a season,*
> *A time for every activity under heaven.*
> *A time to be born and a time to die.*
> *A time to plan and a time to harvest.*
> *A time to kill and a time to heal.*
> *A time to tear down and a*
>   *time to build up.*
> *A time to cry and a time to laugh.*
> *A time to grieve and a time to dance.*
> *A time to scatter stones and a*
>   *time to gather stones.*
> *A time to embrace and a*
>   *time to turn away.*
> *A time to search and a time*
>   *to quit searching.*
> *A time to keep and a time to throw away.*
> *A time to tear and a time to mend.*
> *A time to be quiet and a time to speak.*
> *A time to love and a time to hate.*
> *A time for war and a time for peace.*
>
> Ecclesiastes 3:1-8, NLT

LISA KROEHLER

I love the verse:

> *"A time to cry and a time to laugh.*
> *A time to grieve and a time to dance."*

Lord, help me to laugh and dance more!

CHAPTER 8

TOGETHER WE CAN

Small victories deserve to be celebrated. We finally rented a building for our equipment and vehicles. The employees met there instead of at my house; they were no longer using my washer and dryer. That brought some normalcy to my life.

There was another problem brewing. Although the business was doing well and we were finalizing plans to build a house, I felt like Keith and I were growing distant. Everything was fine when we were with our children, but when we were alone, it was pretty quiet. It just felt like something was missing. We both worked equally hard at making the business successful, but our marriage needed some attention.

In my mind, I just needed to get away for some fresh air. Women joke about running away from home for a few days. But how many actually do it? One Friday afternoon, I did. I do not remember what exactly triggered it, but I told him I was leaving for a couple of days.

"What do you mean you are going away?" he asked, perplexed.

"I need to get away and regroup," I said with a few tears of exasperation. "I just need some alone time. You'll be fine with the kids."

He was stunned that I actually just walked out to my car and drove away. Looking back now, I cannot believe I actually did that. I was dramatic, but at that time, I was losing my grip. After driving around and eating some junk food, I ended up at a friend's house. I knew she understood relationship struggles, and we had many meaningful conversations over the years. I walked up to the door, and when she saw my face, she asked no questions but took me right in. I really had no well-thought-out plan after leaving home. This was unusual behavior for me; I was the chief organizer and planner. I was a fighter who juggled lots of balls and seldom dropped them. I was not a quitter, but right now, I felt like quitting.

At first, all I wanted was coffee and chocolate and someone to cheer me up. I was not looking to hear about the keys to a better marriage. Most of us have heard the tips: Communicate consistently. Respect each other. Don't go to bed angry. You cannot change your spouse, but you can change yourself. And, especially, "Good marriages don't just happen. It takes work!"

Honestly, I really just wanted sympathy. Have you ever had those days when you just want someone who listens and understands your feelings? They aren't telling you that you are wrong or guilty. That's where I was.

Analyzing The Facts

On the second day, my friend and I got into deeper discussions about how couples treat each other. Like most couples, Keith and I were very different. He was a man of few words unless it was a topic he was passionate about - like political issues, gardening, or sports. I had an opinion about almost everything and was not afraid to share it. I was strong-willed and more of an out-front person. He was a diligent guy, working behind the scenes. Don't get me

Don't get me wrong, I loved this man. I was not looking for a way out of my marriage. I just wanted to feel more appreciated and garner more attention than I was getting.

wrong, I loved this man. I was not looking for a way out of my marriage. I just wanted to feel more appreciated and garner more attention than I was getting. Children, business, and life's challenges seemed to get in the way.

I sometimes put roadblocks between us. I could be critical or think I always had the right answer. I was more likely to speak before I really thought through things. Keith usually held his emotions or responded very little. His frustrations exploded about once every three months. Then to top it all off, we worked together every day.

By Saturday evening, I was hoping that Keith was worrying about me and wondering what I was doing. I did not call him. With no cell phones, there was no tracking me down. I would have to apologize for my irresponsible behavior when I returned home, but for now, I was enjoying the alone time. Having a nine-year-old, a six-year-old, and a three-year-old definitely had something to do with my need for quiet moments.

As I sat in the guest room alone that night, I thought about my life and realized how blessed I was. I loved my children and had a man who loved me and sacrificed himself daily. Of course, I knew that all married couples went through rough patches. You realize that two human beings come together and work continuously to overcome their differences. Our love and commitment to each other had bonded us.

Facing Reality

By Sunday, I was ready to go home. As I drove past our church, I saw Keith walking to the car with the kids. They were dressed nicely! Tears welled up in my eyes, knowing he could have opted to stay home and not hassled with getting them ready. He was a good man, and we needed to figure out how we could better connect. When I got home for lunch, everyone was happy to see me. Keith and I hugged but knew there would be some long conversations later.

When we did talk, it was deep and heartfelt. That did not mean we agreed on everything; we wanted to work harder on the gaps between us. So much in life vies for our attention, and it is the little things that sneak in and steal your heart. Improving how we treat and invest in each other had ended up being a lifelong challenge. We knew that we were better together than apart, and it was worth working out our problems. In all transparency, there have been hurtful words said over our thirty-seven years together that we have both regretted. Authentically asking for forgiveness from the Lord and from each other makes all the difference.

LISA KROEHLER

A New Home

By late summer, the concrete house was underway. If there's ever a test of a marriage, it's when you are building a house. Keith spent about a year barely involved in the business. He designed and built the house we still live in today. Except for roofing and drywalling, most of the work was done by him and one other man. Some family members helped from time to time, and my father made all the oak trim inside the house.

It was such a glorious day to move out of the mouse house! We threw away the ragged possessions we had had for years. II Corinthians 5:17, NLT says: *This means that anyone who belongs to Christ has become a new person. The old life is gone; a new life has begun!* A life with Christ is not about possessions like our house, but it is about throwing away the old and putting on the new life that Christ has for us. Just as our new house was not entirely finished when we moved in, Christ certainly was not done with us as a couple. We definitely were a work in progress.

> *Just as our new house was not entirely finished when we moved in, Christ certainly was not done with us as a couple. We definitely were a work in progress.*

NEVER SAY NEVER

TAKEAWAYS FOR LIFE

When you are first married, everything seems positive and possible. Together, you feel like you can conquer the world, and nothing will ever get in the way. And then there is your first disagreement. For me, it was on our honeymoon when I saw a side of Keith I had not seen before. We were walking in a wealthy neighborhood, and he decided to jump a homeowner's fence to investigate their backyard. I was shocked that he would have the audacity to do that. There was even a no trespassing sign. I realized he was someone who liked to color outside the lines. A lot.

Why is it easier to focus on the things we want to change about someone as opposed to focusing on all the great things they bring to our lives? Unfortunately, it is a combination of our humanness and the negativity that pervades our minds. The turmoil we hear and see every day can taint our view of what is good and lovely. I think that carries over into our personal lives such that we often take out our frustrations on those we love most.

How do we overcome a tendency to be critical? First of all, I am guilty of this. Every day, I have to work at seeing the glass half full instead of half empty in everything from my relationship with my husband to facing challenges at work. I don't think I was always like that, but somewhere along the way, it became my thorn.

I have found only one way to overcome the barrage of negativity that attacks my mind. I have to get a fresh perspective every day from reading the Bible. The Word of God shows us who God is. Not only is He a loving God who cares about every detail of our lives, but He is the one who can renew our mind, bring us peace, and give us hope for today and tomorrow.

> *Romans 12:2, NLT says, Don't copy the behavior and customs of this world, but let God transform you into a new person by changing the way you think. Then you will learn to know God's will for you, which is good and pleasing and perfect. When we reflect on His promises and the good plans He has for us, it literally revives our spirit and fills us with hope and expectation. God's Word also strengthens us to keep going, not give up, and not give in to temptation.*

Our mind is a battlefield. I think Philippians 4:8-9, NIV tells us what can help us.

Finally, brothers and sisters, whatever is true, whatever is noble, whatever is right, whatever is pure, whatever is lovely, whatever is admirable—if anything is excellent or praiseworthy—think about such things. Whatever you have learned or received or heard from me or seen in me- put into practice. And the God of peace will be with you.

One of my favorite hymns from the 1970s is "Because He Lives," written by Bill and Gloria Gaither. When you are feeling overwhelmed, battling negativity, fear, and frustration, recall these wonderful words of life.

> "And because He lives, I can face tomorrow
> Because He lives, All fear is gone
> Because I know He holds the future
> And life is worth the living
> > Just because He lives."

CHAPTER 9

SEIZE THE DAY

The next several years of building the business and raising our family were an unforgettable time. I cherish all the memories of parenthood, and I am proud of all of my children for the people they have become. We have been blessed beyond measure, and I am grateful for it all.

Keith and I started going to Florida a couple of weeks every January. Part of it was work-related, and the rest was for pleasure. The beautiful alone times near the ocean always took me down memory lane. I would think about our children and their spouses and our first grandchild, Quinn. I would always start thinking about Mom. When your world slows down, you tend to look at the past.

I remember August of 1999 like it was yesterday. I walked into my parents' house, and Dad was standing there, crying. I had never seen him cry before. He waved me closer and whispered loudly, "Mom has cancer." I was in shock. Mom came into the room, and when I looked into her eyes, I knew right away that it was true. I grabbed her and held her tightly as we both sobbed.

A couple of weeks earlier, the doctors had found a spot on her lung. Now we had the results of the biopsy, and it was lung cancer. Inoperable. How does that happen when your mother is not a smoker? My mind could not process it. Over the next several months, Mom went through grueling chemotherapy treatments. Then the doctors insisted on brain radiation treatments because lung cancer often develops into brain cancer.

Mom had tremendous support from family, friends, and pastors who loved and admired her. She not only believed in prayer, but the Bible was her guide. Hers was marked with highlighters, emphasizing verses that tugged at her heart. She loved and prayed much over her children and grandchildren. I believed that God was going to heal her—why wouldn't He?

At the end of May, Mom was in the hospital in an unconscious state. I read to her, prayed over her, and played worship music in her room. Suddenly, she woke up! She improved, and they moved her into a step-down unit. I just knew that this was the miracle we were hoping for. On my 40th birthday on June 1, Mom held up a *Happy*

Birthday! sign and smiled. Her voice was raspy, so she was not speaking, but the smile said it all.

Saying Goodbye

Just as fast as she had turned around, she was suddenly slipping away. The doctor said that her body was shutting down. He recommended morphine to make her comfortable. Families have such difficult decisions to make in these moments, whether they feel capable of it or not. Mom was only sixty-three years old, and I could not believe this would be the end of her life. My children were small, and I wanted their grandma to see them grow up. And I still needed her! I stood next to her hospital bed, holding her hand and listening to her pastor reading Psalm 23 out loud.

Mom's eyes opened briefly, but I knew she was drifting away. I did not want to hear Psalm 23. It talked about walking through the valley of the shadow of death. I was believing for a miracle, not death.

All of my siblings were there that night. Sometimes, we were crying, while other times, we were laughing and sharing stories. Everyone responds to grief and loss differently. No one is ever prepared for this, especially when it is your own mom.

The next day, she was gone. I grappled with all the questions and feelings that most people ask: why her? Why did Jesus need her now? Why wasn't she healed on earth? I did not get an answer, but I did get comfort, peace, and strength to go on living. The loss was unbearable at times; it took months before I did not cry every time I drove past her house. Because Mom was a believer in Christ, I knew she was with our heavenly Father. She was now healthy and no longer suffering pain.

> *I did not get an answer, but I did get comfort, peace, and strength to go on living.*

I knew that someday I would see her again, but that did not take away the pain I felt. Losing someone dear to you produces heartache. For me, it also produced guilt. As a business owner accustomed to solving problems, I wondered if there was something else I could have done. Was there another treatment I could have found? Another doctor that could have helped? But one of the doctors told me that she had contracted an infection in the hospital that actually took her life, not the lung cancer. What do you do with that kind of information? I could harbor bitterness, become angry, and even try to sue, but that would accomplish nothing.

Although we did not get to see her healed on earth, I still believe in healing. This did not change my faith or beliefs. I do not know why some people are healed here on earth while others are not. That will be a question for our Lord when we see Him one day. But I have seen enough healing in my lifetime to know that Jesus does still heal people today. Therefore, I will continue to pray and believe.

Fighting Through It

Now there I was in Florida in February of 2017. For a few days, I had been experiencing pain in the middle of my back. I figured it was the hard bed I was sleeping on, and I thought I needed a back adjustment. When we returned to Ohio, I went to the chiropractor three times that week. Shortly afterward, we got a phone call that Keith's Aunt Evelyn died, and we needed to fly to Minnesota for the funeral.

The night before the funeral, we stayed at a small town inn. I was barely asleep when I woke up abruptly with that sharp pain again. This time, the pain was spreading across my back and down my shoulders. Keith was sound asleep, and I did not want to wake him up. I sat in the bathroom, fighting the intense pain for what seemed like an hour. Because I have a hiatal hernia, I thought maybe this was related to it. But honestly, it really did feel like an elephant sitting on me.

After the worst of it was over, I lay on the bed and dozed off for a while. The next morning, I never told Keith about the episode. He heard me mention it to his sister the next day. She immediately said, "Maybe you were having a heart attack!" That thought had never crossed my mind.

After the funeral, our flight was delayed three hours because of tornados. When we finally boarded, we sat on the tarmac for another two hours because of the storms. I do not like flying, anyway, but sitting in the dark while it is storming really produces anxiety. We finally landed in Chicago at one a.m., and we missed our flight to Columbus, Ohio.

Cots were lined up in the airport for all of us to lay on while the storms raged outside. Suddenly, a policeman ran in and told us all to get away from the windows because a tornado was headed toward us. We all hid inside of empty restaurants and waited for the storm to clear. It was hard to believe that so much commotion could happen on one trip. After finally getting to Columbus, we drove two hours to our house. Keith started unpacking; then he came into the living room and told me he wanted to take me to the hospital for a checkup. This was coming from a man who never went to a doctor voluntarily for anything. I resisted his request because I just wanted to go to sleep.

"Lisa, If I don't take you to the hospital and something happens, the kids will never forgive me," he pleaded.

I finally gave in, and it was a good thing that I did. I needed emergency triple bypass heart surgery. The horrific pain was from a widow-maker heart attack. I was told that only 12% of people who have a widow-maker heart attack outside of a hospital actually survive. My cardiologist said, "You should have died in the hotel or in the airport. You should not have survived. The Good Lord must not be done with you yet."

> *"You should have died in the hotel or in the airport. You should not have survived. The Good Lord must not be done with you yet."*

Months after my recovery, I wrote my adult children this letter. It was probably the most meaningful piece I have ever written.

> *Dear family,*
>
> *Intensive care was very lonely and overwhelming. Tubes extended out of my chest, and the worst was the tube that went down my windpipe. I could hardly swallow, and I felt like I was choking the*

entire night. I kept reminding myself that I only needed to make it through the night. I tried to think of every scripture I could and recalled the words to worship songs.

I pleaded to the Lord to help me through the agony. I knew they had cut my chest open, broken my sternum, taken a vein out of my leg, hooked me up to a heart-lung machine, and stopped my heart from beating. How this all works, I don't know, but I knew I had been through a lot. My breastbone was put back together with wire that will forever stay in my body.

I share these details to say that none of us ever knows what we may have to go through. There are no guarantees that we'll avoid great pain or sorrow. The only guarantee we have is that the Lord will be there with us, holding our hand through it all. But the good news is that the morning does come! I made it through that very dark night, and at 7 a.m. when a new nurse came in, I begged her to take the tube out of my throat. When it was removed and I could swallow again, a sense of relief and even joy filled me.

A simple act meant the world to me! I knew I was going to make it even though there was so much more to go through, including having all the tubes pulled out of my chest. But knowing I had made it through such an agonizing night reassured me that I was going to be okay.

When your father walked in later that morning and saw me sitting up in the chair with all the chest tubes removed, he began to cry. He had not expected that after seeing me in such a dire state the evening before. But it is a process—there is no instant healing. I had to endure a lot before I even made it home.

None of us knows what the future will bring. Of course, we pray that it's all great and wonderful, and much of it will be. But there may be some dark days when we are just trying to make it through the night without giving up. Know that the Lord will walk with you through everything if you let Him. The key is letting Him. Going through a near-death experience forever changed me. I hope I never forget what I felt, especially that first night because it's

LISA KROEHLER

a constant reminder that God is the God of Second Chances. And Joy does come in the morning.

Love, Mom

NEVER SAY NEVER

TAKEAWAYS FOR LIFE

After my open heart surgery, I wondered why the Lord gave me a second chance at life. I was fifty-seven when I had the heart attack. My nurses were amazed at my story of survival after such a severe attack, coupled with the anxiety I encountered in the airport. All I can say is that I am so grateful to be alive and experience life with my four grandchildren, Quinn, Jade, Jude, and Max.

When you realize that you were so near death, you cannot help but ask questions. Why was I kept on earth? Is there something I am to accomplish that I have not yet done? I definitely find myself contemplating my life and choices much more deeply.

A second chance to me is the opportunity to live a life of renewed purpose. This is not a one-time decision—it actually is daily. Every day I have to decide who and what I am going to serve. What am I wanting to accomplish this very day? But greater than that, am I asking God what He wants me to accomplish? What is He showing me through the Bible I read and the prayers that I whisper? Facing death has made me more sensitive to His Holy Spirit and the direction He affords me.

The good news for all of us is that God gives us more than just second chances in our everyday lives. His love, mercy, and forgiveness are unending. The Bible is full of stories about real people who were given second chances. That same goodness is offered to each of us.

> *Because of the Lord's great love we are not consumed, for his compassions never fail. They are new every morning; great is your faithfulness.* Lamentations 3:22-23, NIV

> *If we confess our sins, he is faithful and just to forgive us our sins and to cleanse us from all unrighteousness.* 1 John 1:9, NIV

God does not put a limit on loving us, forgiving us, or rescuing us. He makes a way when there seems to be no way.

CHAPTER 10

COUNTING THE COSTS

When we said "I DO" in marriage over thirty-seven years ago, we had no idea we would end up being business partners for over thirty-two years. In fact, had I known that then, I might not have jumped on board. Owning a business together is an exciting adventure as you work toward a shared vision and shared challenges. You are building something together that hopefully has long-lasting benefits and perhaps even generational significance.

BUT...

It is not for the faint of heart. Owning and running a business with your spouse takes a lot of sacrifice, grit, humbleness, and determination... and, of course, commitment. That sounds just like marriage, doesn't it? That's why I call business ownership with your spouse a double marriage. You already deal with those challenges in marriage; now double that when you go into business together. I am not trying to discourage you from a business partnership because it has been a great blessing to us. But sometimes, people dive into something without counting the cost.

Learning And Thriving

Over the years, we have learned a lot from running a business together, and much of it has come through our mistakes. First of all, no one really knows what you are fully getting into in the beginning, especially if you are starting the business from scratch. In 1992 when we started this journey, we did not have the internet, so there was no Googling to find home service business advice from entrepreneurs.

In some ways, that was good. We did not have preconceived ideas or someone else's business plan that we were trying to mimic. We had to figure everything out ourselves, mainly by trial and error, life experiences, and common sense. Common sense is underrated sometimes, and the world would be a better place if more people tapped into it.

In the beginning, it was less complicated because we did not have employees. We were a sole proprietorship just looking for window cleaning work for one person. Fast forward to today, and we have many employees. There is a great sense of responsibility for the people in your company. When you start a business in your thirties, and now you are in your sixties, there definitely is a protectiveness that wells up within you—you want to make sure that everyone and everything is alright. You have been the caretaker for so long and have been responsible for so many people over the years that it really is difficult to relax and let go. But that time is now nearing for us. My son, Josh, is now the Chief Operations Officer and future owner of this seven-figure company. But Keith and I still feel the weight of that ownership responsibility as we have for three decades.

People start businesses for various reasons, usually because they just want to work for themselves instead of an employer. When we started ours, it was for survival. My husband knew how to clean windows professionally, and he could make more money on his own than at his other

> *Common sense is underrated sometimes, and the world would be a better place if more people tapped into it.*

job opportunities back then. Providing for your family is a great motivator to succeed in business.

As we grew and started adding employees (we originally said we would never have employees), we realized that we had so much more to learn in order to grow and sustain the business. The buck stops with you, the owners; sometimes, that means evening phone calls dealing with employee problems or unhappy clients. When you own a 12,000-square-foot business building, it may mean alarms going off in the middle of the night or needing to set up heaters in the shop to avoid broken water pipes. For years, there were no other managers in the company except us... no one else to shoulder the after-hours responsibilities.

After thinking about the challenges we have had as spouses and owners over these years, I have written down a few thoughts on how to make your business run more smoothly. We all know that tough times make tough people. More than that, a love for each other bound with your love for God is what keeps you together. No amount of money or success will ever do that.

NEVER SAY NEVER

Is Running A Business Together A Good Fit For You?

Assess your strengths and weaknesses. Are you both highly motivated, eager to learn, and have the ability to stand strong under pressure? Can you be a tough leader and yet be flexible and admit when you are wrong? Are you hard-working, committed, and ready to tackle the stress that working together can and will bring? Can you pivot when you need to, and do you see you and your spouse equally sharing the workload? The thrill of having your own business will often be overshadowed by the above challenges; you need to be willing to fight for what you have and want.

Set Boundaries And Stay In Your Lane

Each couple has to analyze what they are best at and figure out their partner's job responsibilities. Then let each other do their job without being micromanaged. Keith and I are very opposite when it comes to our strengths and gifts, so it was pretty obvious what our jobs should be. My problem was micromanaging. I would get out of my lane and try to tell him how he should fix the problems that were his responsibilities. Ouch! That definitely steps on toes and causes more stress. After all, what do I really know about fixing purified water systems? I often have a problem restraining myself from giving my input when it is not needed. Yes, that was my challenge in our marriage also.

Decide Who Will Make the Final Decisions

Someone has to be the go-to person making the final decisions in a business, even if you both are discussing the options. I am talking about the bigger decisions on finances, employee and HR issues, and all the emergency problems that pop up. In our business, it is me. If it is related to a crew in the field or a problem on a job site, then it is Keith. Most matters in the office have fallen under my jurisdiction, and he has always respected that. Or maybe he is just glad that he does not have to deal with it!

Do Not Become Easily Offended

Do not fall prey to petty disagreements. You may feel that your spouse is questioning your authority or business expertise when they are asking challenging questions. Do not immediately feel offended or assume they doubt your abilities. Perhaps they are just trying to better assess the situation and make sure that, as a team, you are making the best decisions possible.

I would love to say that Keith and I do not ever have this problem, but that is not true. Yes, you would think we should be above it because we also have a personal, intimate relationship as husband and wife. The truth is that all people who work together, regardless of whether they are married or not, can become defensive and get their feathers ruffled when people question their motives or decisions. We all have insecurities and vulnerabilities. Learning to listen to each other's suggestions without feeling criticized or doubted would help all our relationships.

Stay Committed but Review Your Business Relationship

If one of you is losing the desire and passion to be in business together, you need to talk about it honestly. I have learned that there are seasons in life, and not everything is meant to last forever. Except MARRIAGE. Just because you started out in busi-

I have learned that there are seasons in life, and not everything is meant to last forever. Except MARRIAGE.

ness together does not mean that it is meant to be a lifelong adventure for both of you. I was a media communicator before I got involved in owning a window-cleaning business. Of course, I have been able to use my marketing, writing, and media skills in our company, but there was a time about fifteen years ago when I was really questioning whether I wanted to stay in business with my husband. There was a lot of stress, and it was hard separating work and family life. I wondered if I was missing out on something else in life, and I really had to analyze where I was and what I wanted for our future.

It was something I had to work through, and as I laid out the pros and cons of being in business together, I realized that there were way more benefits to working together than not. That was my decision, and it may not be yours. Always be honest with your spouse and yourself, and continually pray about all things.

Respect Each Other Even When You Do Not Agree

If all of us who are married were truly honest, we would admit that we have lost control in some marital disagreements. Believe me, that absolutely happens when you work together. The key is to take a step back and not let unrelated matters get thrown into the conflict. ("You never ask me how I am feeling," or "I need you to help more with the kids.") Don't make it a melting pot of problems in your discussion. Stick to the matter at hand and try to calmly explain your viewpoint while certainly respecting your spouse's thoughts, even if they are vastly different from yours.

Keith and I try not to have difficult discussions in the office because there are many ears listening. We step outside to talk about a pressing issue we are disagreeing on or wait until later when we both have cooled down. I only remember a few times when we were talking way too loudly in the office (okay, I'll say the word—fighting), and I regretted it. Let me be clear: there have been times in our home when we have raised our voices. I regret those, too, but we have always tried to be respectful to each other.

Guard Your Words and Your Heart

Words are powerful and can either build up or tear down. In marriage, we all know how easily a little tiff can turn into a hurtful argument very quickly. It is no different in business, whether we are talking with a partner or having a conversation with other team members. Words become weapons, especially when we are already frustrated, and let them run out of our mouths without thinking.

Build Trust

Do what you say you intend to do. Believe in your spouse and the hard work and talents they bring to the business. Let them know how much you appreciate their sacrifices, long hours, and the stress they have to endure. I know there have been times when I made Keith feel like I did not trust him and his abilities or decision-making. In reality, I was feeling insecure in my own abilities but managed to lash out with distrust instead.

If you sabotage your spouse at work, you have sabotaged him in your marriage. We are all human and cannot separate our hurt as much as we would like to or think we can. Again, this is a double marriage, and what we do and say at work to our spouses will be tough to forget when we head home.

> *If you sabotage your spouse at work, you have sabotaged him in your marriage... and what we do and say at work to our spouses will be tough to forget when we head home.*

NEVER SAY NEVER

You and Your Spouse are Separate People

You have different personalities, talents, and ways of processing information. You will not always be on the same page because you will not always see things from the same perspective. You both are unique; that is how God designed you. It is the beauty of working together. You both have something to offer, and because you are unique, your business vision and plans will be fuller and more complete. But that does not mean that there is no room for improvement in how you treat each other.

We often want to use the excuse that we argue because we are so different. Although there is some truth here, we can always improve how we approach sensitive subjects or differing viewpoints. Learning to love each other despite our differences is a long process that continues throughout our marriages. Learning to work with each other harmoniously is a long process too.

Many arrows are shot at us every day, and sometimes, you get tired of dodging them in your business. You need to take a step back and get some perspective and alone time. For me, that means prayer and worship music. I have to get my head and heart together; that means I have to remove myself from the stressors of the business. Remember that no man is an island. We need each other—other believers who can encourage and lift us up when we are feeling down. We especially need strength, wisdom, and insight from the Lord to do and say the right things to our spouses in every situation. Make sure you come away with Him.

Communicate, Don't Stuff it Inside

Everyone deals with conflict differently. I am someone who wants to talk right away about the problem at hand. My husband internalizes the problem and lets the conflict build until it explodes at some point. For most of us, the way we handle conflict started when we were children and watched our parents deal with it. Most people would agree that bottling up your feelings can be harmful all the way around. Sorry, Dear, I do think that communicating right away is important!

Don't Hang Onto Past Mistakes

There will always be failures and disappointments. Do not dwell on them, and resist the urge to place the blame on your spouse. Everyone is going to mess up and make a wrong decision. Holding onto grudges and bringing up the failures over and over only leads to destruction. Talk out your problems together and move your marriage and your business forward. Come up with a plan that you both can agree on.

You Need Personal Space

Do not share a small office together: you both need your space and privacy. We learned right away that we cannot be around each other all day at work and then at home all evening long. During the day, Keith is usually out in the shop or on the road selling while I am in the office. There needs to be some separation from each other. After our evening dinner, he often goes downstairs to watch television, and I stay upstairs. We end up together for a while in the living room as our way of saying that we are still ONE.

Obviously, this does not happen every day, but it is more likely to happen when we have both undergone more stress at work or when we have been in many meetings together that day. Being alone is a good thing as long as you always come together in the end.

LISA KROEHLER

Escape Often and Unplug

Make sure you develop friendships that have nothing to do with your business. You have to get away from it, laugh with friends, and talk about your faith and family. Take frequent mini trips as a couple, even if it is dinner out and a night in a nice hotel. A change of environment and atmosphere is so important when you are business owners. When our children were young, so was our business. Keith arranged a trade-out with a local Holiday Inn that had a beautiful indoor pool. We would clean windows there once a month in exchange for a one-night stay.

We often saved up our nights and brought other friends along for a quick getaway with their kids. Our grown children have fond memories of those simple times, and so do we.

Remember Why You Went Into Business Together

On those days when it feels like everything is going wrong at work, reminisce with your spouse as to why you went into business in the first place. You will remember the early challenges you faced but also the excitement of planning your future together—just like you did when you were dating. Recall how far you have come in your business and how grateful you are for all it has brought to your family.

Set Boundaries on Work Conversations

This one is not easy. Our plan is that by the time we start eating dinner, we need to be done discussing work. It was easier when the children still lived at home because we made more of an effort. The problem is that many issues come up at the end of the work day that are not resolved right away. When you own a business, there are no time clocks. But you can purposely do your best to follow your guidelines. Again, there is no perfect plan, so always strive to protect yourselves.

Your Marriage Must Come First

You and your spouse have to decide how to take care of your relationship outside of the workplace. One of the hardest things to deal with is shedding any frustrations you had both encountered at work. There is nothing magical about this; it just takes effort and commitment to protect your marriage. Will you fail sometimes? Absolutely.

Even after all of these years of working together, this is still a challenge for us.

Be Deliberate In Resolving Conflict

I don't recommend that you sit back and let the chips fall where they may. You can avoid pitfalls by being proactive in problem-solving and discussing strategies. When it is just the two of you in the business, it is easier than when you have employees and a big payroll. Stress mounts, and it can be overwhelming. Remember when you had your first fight in your marriage? You realized that it was going to take work to overcome your differences. Now you're in business together, and you realize that it will be the same amount of work as in a marriage. You two have to stand together to face whatever comes at you.

A Three Stranded Cord is Not Easily Broken

Ecclesiastes 4:12, NLT says, *A person standing alone can be attacked and defeated, but two can stand back-to-back and conquer. Three are even better, for a triple braided cord is not easily broken.* You and your spouse are stronger when the Lord is the center of your marriage and your business relationship. The three of you can do amazing things in your business and in other people's lives. The Lord wants to bless your business so that you can be a blessing to others. There are so many wonderful scriptures that talk about the blessings of God.

> *But blessed is the one who trusts in the Lord, whose confidence is in Him. They will be like a tree planted by the water that sends out its roots by the stream. It does not fear when heat comes; its leaves are always green. It has no worries in a year of drought and never fails to bear fruit.* Jeremiah 17:7-8, NIV

> *Taste and see that the Lord is good; blessed is the one who takes refuge in Him.* Psalm 34:8, NIV

> *For I know the plans I have for you, declares the Lord, plans to prosper you and not to harm you, plans to give you hope and a future.* Jeremiah 29:11, NIV

LISA KROEHLER

TAKEAWAYS FOR LIFE

During the spring of 2020 when COVID-19 first ravaged the world, a song called "The Blessing" also traveled the globe and proclaimed a blessing over families everywhere. Sung by Kari Jobe and her husband Cody Carnes and Elevation Worship, the song focuses on Numbers 6:24-26, NLT: *May the Lord bless you and protect you. May the Lord smile on you and be gracious to you. May the Lord show his favor and give you his peace.* Over and over they sing, *"He is for you, He is for you."*

If there is anything I can say today to encourage you in your marriage and your business, it is that God is for you. He wants to strengthen your marriage, He wants your business to succeed, He wants to bless you, He wants to protect you, and He wants to give you peace. God is for you. But as always, we can choose to believe it and accept that blessing, or we can resist.

When we stubbornly say that we can do life alone or succeed alone, we are miserably wrong, and our lives will reflect it. Does that mean we will never endure trials or face hardships in our lives? No, it does not. But that is how we grow as people and how God molds us to become more like Jesus. The best business and marriage advice I could ever give anyone is simply, "Say YES to Jesus Christ and walk with Him. You will never have to walk alone."

CHAPTER 11

A LIFE OF GRATITUDE

Our business grew greatly in 2019. At our Christmas party, I remember thinking that 2020 would certainly be a banner year. Then there was something that changed everything. COVID-19. None of us will ever forget what that means. There will be stories to tell our grandchildren and great-grandchildren. The pain and loss that families suffered during the pandemic still haunt many. We all were affected by it one way or another. Like most companies in 2020, we were focusing on surviving in the midst of shutdowns and unknowns. We weathered all the storms and learned a lot about pivoting and frugality. Then in November 2021, Keith and I got the virus, and it hit us like a ton of bricks.

LISA KROEHLER

In Sickness And In Health

I had every flu symptom hit me within a few hours while Keith mainly had severe coughing with body aches. Like everyone else, we experienced severe exhaustion. There would be no Thanksgiving dinner this year. When my kids stopped to check on us a few days after it all started, they were shocked to see how bad we were, especially me. I could not get out of bed and was getting dehydrated. Somehow, Jessica was able to get through to our regenerative disease doctor's office on a Sunday.

The nurse practitioner recommended that she stay all night and wake me up periodically to test my oxygen numbers. They were running low. The next day, Keith and I somehow drove two hours to get treatment. Because we had COVID, they treated us in the parking lot with intravenous fluids and stem cell therapy to help our respiratory problems. I was hooked up to oxygen.

That night, I went downhill fast. Treatments take time to work, and I was already in bad shape. Courtney, a friend and Physician Assistant at a local hospital, had been keeping in touch with Jessica. She frankly became an angel for us during this crisis. Jessica was on the phone with her that night, updating her on my oxygen numbers and lethargic condition. With my heart history, I was at a great risk of slipping quickly. Courtney told her that I needed to get to the hospital.

"I am not going," I told my kids as I was lying in bed. "I will never get out of there alive."

I had fear about going because we knew a couple of people who had died in the hospital with COVID. I absolutely did not want to be put on a ventilator. Even though I felt somewhat delirious, I was listening to my family's conversations. My son set me straight. "Mom, an ambulance is coming, and you are going to the hospital. If you don't, there's a good chance you are not going to make it. We are going to be with you," he promised.

The paramedics carried me out of the house on a stretcher. The evening air was cold, and snow was spitting onto my face. Through the wide open door, I could see Keith sitting on the couch. He showed no emotion; he did not speak and looked miserable. Although he was not going to the hospital, he was very sick and seemed forgotten by everyone. I wondered if I would ever see him again.

The ride in the ambulance was surreal. The voices of the paramedics were clear and yet distant as they called in my vital signs. I found out later that I also had acute kidney failure, probably from dehydration. I felt a total lack of control over anything, yet I felt strangely calm. I truly knew the peace that can only come from God.

They wheeled me into the hospital emergency area, where I had to stay for hours because the hospital was full. When I finally was moved to a room, I felt like they had taken me to the attic bedroom in Grandma's house. It was a specially designed room for COVID patients and the epitome of a claustrophobic's nightmare. The ceiling was low, and there were no windows. I was definitely isolated. If Jessica and Josh had not taken turns staying with me, I think I would have emotionally lost it. Every part of me felt like I was holding on by a thread.

I wish I could say that I was praying and full of faith, but at that point, I was not. I was weak and in and out of awareness. This is when you definitely need the prayers of your friends and family to sustain you. And they did. Friends made scripture signs, and my kids posted them in my room. Although I don't remember the details, I knew they were there. My daughter was the point person for getting the word out and contacting healthcare providers who knew alternative protocols for severe COVID patients. She heard from people all over the country who offered helpful information.

After being in the hospital for six days, I had improved enough to be released. I was still sick and on oxygen 24 hours a day, but I was thrilled to go home.

Keith was better but not quite himself yet. Within a few hours after being home, I was struggling with my memory. My kids were quizzing me about all kinds of things, and I could not answer clearly. What was my wedding date? Who is the president? How old am I? The simplest of questions I could not answer, and they were about ready to take me back to the hospital. After calling a nurse, we found out that I probably needed higher concentrations of oxygen like I had in the hospital and a stronger steroid. It was a scary couple of hours, but after making adjustments, I was thinking and talking normally again.

For weeks, I spent most of my time in a recliner, wearing a full oxygen mask that allowed higher concentrations and rates of oxygen flow as compared to a nasal cannula. For most people, a normal pulse oximeter reading for your oxygen is 96%-100%. In my worst state, before I went to the hospital, it was in the mid 80s range. We were told that below 92% is dangerous.

Jessica and Josh had put their lives on hold to focus on me for the last couple of weeks. Keith finally turned the corner and could help again. It was Christmas season, and my youngest son, Justin, was flying in from California to celebrate an early Christmas with us. He was pretty shocked to see my condition since he had only been hearing about me through phone calls.

We always opened presents in the lower level of the house where we had a fireplace. I was determined that I was going to make it down there. That meant my two sons would have to practically carry me down the stairs—oxygen tubes and all. My spirits were uplifted, watching my grandchildren opening gifts. That joy was indescribable. Afterward, I ended up crawling up the stairs because I was so weak. I felt like an invalid and realized I was not going to rebound quickly from COVID. In fact, I was on oxygen for many months, and my brain fog lasted even longer.

The Goodness Of God

Listening to Christian music helped me through the long days. All winter long, I watched videos of CeCe Winans singing songs from her new album, *Believe For It*. Words such as "*They say this mountain can't be moved, They say these chains will never break, But they don't know You like we do, There is power in Your Name.*" I would play the videos over and over to get the words deep into my soul and my foggy brain. I believe that what we hear and see affects us. Still, whenever I hear "The Goodness of God," I am brought to tears. It talks about how God's mercy never fails us. He holds us in His hands. All my life, God has been faithful. No matter what I have gone through or how low I have felt, God has always been with me. When I look back at my life, I see that God has led me through the fire. In my darkest nights, He has been closer than anyone else could be. I especially love this verse:

"And all my life You have been faithful
And all my life You have been so, so good
With every breath that I am able
Oh, I will sing of the goodness of God."

"With every breath that I am able"—that took on new meaning as I struggled to breathe. All my life, He has been so good to me. His goodness was running after me. I was only alive because God decided twice that He was not done with me yet. I am now fully recovered from COVID, and I am so grateful for my life.

"And all my life You have been faithful
And all my life You have been so, so good
With every breath that I am able
Oh, I will sing of the goodness of God."

For years, I wanted to write a book about the journey that Keith and I have been on. I did not have a journal or set of notes to refer to when I started writing in January of 2023. In fact, I was still dealing with remnants of brain fog and wondered if I could really undertake such a project.

Going back in time to write about situations that occurred as much as thirty-eight years before was challenging.

I started by writing timelines and the details I could remember. I later wrote pages about the life-altering situations that you have read here. Sometimes, I would quiz my husband to make sure I had the story straight, but going over some of the past details was hard for Keith. Some things he wanted to forget. I would always tell him that this story of our lives together was handwritten by God. We need to share the ups and downs of our lives so we can hopefully inspire others. I especially wanted people to see that none of us have to walk through life alone. God always has an outstretched hand waiting patiently for us to grab onto it.

After all I had been through physically, I decided that I would stay working part-time from home. Our son was now running the company's day to day operations, and I was always available to help with projects. I figured I would have plenty of time to write the book now. After all, I had two near-death experiences in the last six years—doesn't that give me some leeway?

NEVER SAY NEVER

Life Throws Curveballs

As life always does, it throws curveballs that you were not expecting. Right now, I am back in our business full-time because they need me. This is just the way life is—the way business ownership is. There will always be challenges to face and opportunities to help others. As leaders, we rise to the occasion and do what we need to do. It also reminds me that I do not run on my own strength. As a Christian, my strength truly comes from the Lord. We all have had times when we wondered whether we could even get out of bed in the morning to face what the day would bring. But we can never give up. God has a purpose for each of us, no matter who we are or what stage of life we are in. Keep moving forward.

I talked to someone recently who had retired at age sixty-five, but now she struggles with not having a purpose. We don't have to have a job or career to give us purpose, but we do need a reason to get up in the morning—we need a reason to live. There are many opportunities to serve people, and there is always a shortage of volunteers in nonprofits. There are many ways to share our faith in Christ. Think about the lost world around us and how we have answers for people seeking peace in their lives. As the world continues to spin out of control, we know that He is the only hope we have.

As I talked about in Chapter 9, "Seize The Day," make the most of where you are in life. Break out of the mundane and grab hold of enjoying life. None of us are guaranteed another day. Do not let the sadness and evil you see around you suffocate you. Rise up! Find your passion and your purpose in this phase of your life. Share your life story with your children and grandchildren. They need to know where you came from and what you have gone through.

No one has a perfect life. No one avoids heartache, hardship, or physical and mental struggles. There will always be disappointments and failures; often, we want to hide these from others because we are embarrassed or ashamed. But others need to hear your story because it can make a difference in their life.

But others need to hear your story because it can make a difference in their life.

I am constantly reminded that we cannot coast through our later years and sit on the sidelines. We are still needed on the playing field. Your level of involvement may look different than it did ten years ago, but people still need you. God still needs you. We all are His hands and feet, and He can use us to help others.

NEVER SAY NEVER

Matters Of The Heart

This reminds me of the many conversations I had with my dad the last weeks of his life in 2022. At age eighty-six, he was probably the happiest person I ever knew. Not because of fortune and fame but because he lived a life walking with God and living life to the fullest. He loved to tell stories and make people laugh. His laughter was infectious, and he never knew a stranger. He would hop into his red Ford 150 pickup and drive an unplanned route in Ohio or Indiana to visit antique stores and barns. His purpose was to talk with strangers, share stories, and end up laughing together. It was a pretty simple life plan.

Dad often talked to me about the phases in life that we all go through. He told me the story of when he gave up drinking beer once and for all in his mid-forties. He said that God had brought him to a place of total surrender. Dad knew that this decision would change his life and his family's life forever. It did. As a young child, I still remember watching him pour bottles of beer down the kitchen sink.

"We have all of these seasons we go through in life before we ultimately get to where we are going to end up—that's when we face death," I recorded Dad saying. "And in the twinkling of an eye, you'll be where you're going to end up. You don't know when it's going to happen; it just happens… For one person, it could be age forty-two; for your mom, it was age sixty-three. But in the end, you will be going to one of two places (Heaven or Hell), and it's for eternity. That's forever."

Think about it. Our cars, houses, and retirement funds do not matter in the end. We all are going to die sometime, and when we do, we are all at the same level. We take nothing with us and will end up in one of two places: Heaven or Hell. Where we end up is really up to us because we have free will. We decide whether we are going to believe the Bible (the Word of God). The Bible teaches us that Jesus Christ was the Son of God, born to the Virgin Mary, lived a sinless life, then died on the cross for all of mankind's sins. Jesus was resurrected from the dead and paid our penalty so that we who believe in Him and repent will live with Him forever in eternity. That is the Good News of the Gospel.

Because my faith is the most important thing I possess, I would be remiss not to be bold and ask you, "Do you really know Jesus Christ as your Lord and Savior?" It is not a religion, and it has nothing to do with church attendance. This is strictly a heart matter.

> Acts 16:30-31, NIV says, *"He then brought them out and asked, 'Sirs, what must I do to be saved?'" They replied, "Believe in the*

Lord Jesus, and you will be saved—you and your household."

Romans 10:9-10, NLT says, "If you openly declare that Jesus is Lord and believe in your heart that God raised him from the dead, you will be saved. For it is by believing in your heart that you are made right with God, and it is by openly declaring your faith that you are saved."

As I have shared in this book, at the age of sixteen, I asked Jesus to become the Lord of my Life. My life has been full because of my faith and walk with Christ. Have I been perfect? Absolutely not. I have stumbled and even fallen at times in my life when I took my eyes off of the One who not only created me but died for me. Thankfully, God's grace has been sufficient for me. Grace means undeserved favor. Grace cannot be earned. It is something that is freely given. I did not deserve anything that God had given me.

There are better days ahead for you if you invite Christ into your life. Without Him holding your hand, life is rugged and tough. That does not mean you will not have any problems in life. It means that you will have someone walking with you, even carrying you when you need it most. My prayer for you is that you will surrender your life and heart to Christ today simply by believing in Him, repenting of your sins, and asking Him to be the Lord of your life. I guarantee that your life will never be the same.

At the end of Dad's life, he talked about the goodness of God. He was thankful for his family and the many opportunities God gave him to help people. Dad acknowledged that we all have challenges in life, but the goodness outweighs the bad. He summed it up best: "We have a better life coming in heaven. Yep, we have a better life coming."

NEVER SAY NEVER

TAKEAWAYS FOR LIFE

Everyone's life story has good times and sad times. Keith and I have had happy moments and times of laughter. But if we are honest, it is the tough experiences of life that we really learn from. I hope our story, with recurring themes of hope, resilience, perseverance, and faith in God, has touched your heart and encouraged you in whatever season of life you find yourself in. You can have confident peace in the midst of a storm. You can cling to hope through your faith. You can get back up when you have been knocked down. God is for you and not against you. You and your spouse can have a successful business together by staying true to God and each other and by staying focused on what really matters. Keith and I have been richly blessed in our family life and in our window cleaning company of 32 years. All that we have and all that we have done, we give credit to our Lord. One of the most meaningful songs to me is "Through it All," written and sung by Andrae Crouch.

> "I've had many tears and sorrow
> I've had questions for tomorrow
> There've been times I didn't
>   know right from wrong
> But in every situation

God gave me blessed consolation
That my trials come to only
    make me strong.
So I thank God for the mountains
And I thank Him for the valleys
And I thank Him for the storms
    He's brought me through
For if I'd never had a problem
I'd never know God could solve them
I'd never know what faith in
    His word could do
That's the reason I say that
Through it all, Oh Through it all
Oh, I've learned to trust in Jesus
I've learned to trust in God
Oh let me tell you Through it All
Oh through it all
Oh, I've learned to depend
    upon His word..."

ABOUT THE AUTHOR

Lisa Kroehler has been writing stories since she was ten years old. A graduate of Bowling Green State University with a bachelor's degree in news editorial journalism, she has worked in newspapers, magazines, and television.

She is the CEO and co-owner of IDW Window & Roof Cleaning LLC and Creative Services of Ohio LLC in Lima, Ohio. Lisa and her husband, Keith, started the window cleaning business 32 years ago, and it continues to grow. With four grandchildren and hoping for more, Lisa wants to inspire future generations to walk in faith and hope.

Lisa was an author in Illuminate Volume 2: Difference Makers Shining Through Their Stories by Michelle Prince. To contact Lisa, email her at lisakroehler@gmail.com.

Visit her websites: www.idowindowsllc.com and www.lisakroehler.com.

www.ingramcontent.com/pod-product-compliance
Lightning Source LLC
Chambersburg PA
CBHW032047150426
43194CB00006B/447